K

£4:99

THE COTTAGE
HOMES
OF ENGLAND

THE COTTAGE
HOMES
OF ENGLAND

Helen Allingham and Stewart Dick

Bracken Books
LONDON

First published 1909 by Edward Arnold, London.

This edition published by Bracken Books,
a division of Bestseller Publications Ltd.,
Princess House, 50 Eastcastle Street, London W1N 7AP, England
and Copyright © Bracken Books 1984.
Third reprint 1986
ISBN 0 946495 10 6

Printed and bound by Kultura, Hungary

PREFACE

In this volume I have attempted to summarise the history of the old English cottages and farmhouses which still adorn the villages and lanes of the countryside, and in some measure to trace the causes which resulted in their present form. Without entering into undue technicalities I have also endeavoured to explain clearly their system of construction.

On the historical side I have consulted many authorities, and on the architectural side am particularly indebted to the authors and illustrators of Messrs. Batsford's excellent series on old English cottages, to Mr. Ralph Nevill, F.S.A., Mr. S. O. Addy, and many others.

The rest has been supplied from a personal acquaintance with many of these quiet places and old buildings, now alas growing fewer, whose subtle charm speaks so eloquently in Mrs. Allingham's pictures.

STEWART DICK.

' The house which a man has built seems to express his character and stand for him before the world.'

GEORGE DOUGLAS.

CONTENTS

My special thanks are due to Mr. Batsford for permission in preparing this book to make use of the following volumes in his excellent 'Old Cottage Series': 'Old Cottages and Farmhouses in the Cotswold District,' by E. Guy Dawber; 'Old Cottages and Farmhouses in Kent and Sussex,' by the same author; and 'Old Cottages and Farmhouses in Surrey,' by W. Curtis Green.

Stewart Dick

PUBLISHER'S NOTE

For this edition, the illustrations have been re-grouped and given plate numbers, but remain in their original order. The references in the facsimile text therefore no longer apply, and footnotes have been added to direct the reader to the corresponding illustration.

LIST OF ILLUSTRATIONS

and owners of the original pictures at the time of the first edition

THE COTTAGE HOMES
OF ENGLAND

CHAPTER I

ON COTTAGES IN GENERAL

'The lovely cottage in the guardian nook
. . . with its own dear brook,
Its own pasture, almost its own sky.'

WORDSWORTH.

IF one were asked what is the most typical figure in England to-day, it would be difficult to answer the question. There seems to be no type which stands for the modern Englishman.

John Bull is little more than a name now, and he does not truly represent, even in caricature, the English people. He is like the figure-head which used to adorn the old wooden walls of England, fixed to the prow of a modern deep-sea tramp. He looks rather out of date and certainly much out of place, and one would fain see him relegated to the lumber of the ship-breaker's yard.

For, representing as he does the bluff farmer of

Georgian days, he belongs to the old era of agriculture and hand-labour, which has passed away. But in these shifting and transitory times we have not been able to evolve a new type to take his place. 'A nation of shopkeepers,' said Napoleon. Perhaps he was right, and our most typical figure to-day is the grocer. But he is of little use as a type. His only distinctive feature is that he has none. He sells anything and everything. Hardly an article in his shop is native produce; he is a shopkeeper and a tradesman, and nothing more. Perhaps it was not always so. Perhaps a touch of the glamour which still clings to the merchant and makes Antonio with his ventures afloat in many seas so picturesque a figure, once surrounded the grocer, and he himself was touched with the poetic possibilities of his position. Mr. G. K. Chesterton eloquently remarks to him: 'I can imagine what it must be to sit all day as you do surrounded with wares from all the ends of the earth, from strange seas that we have never sailed, and strange ports that we could not even picture. No Eastern king ever had such argosies or such cargoes coming from the sunrise and the sunset, and Solomon in all his glory was not enriched like one of you. India is at your elbow, China is before you,

Demerara is behind you, America is above your head, and at this very moment, like some old Spanish admiral, you hold Tunis in your hands,' and these gorgeous words make him appear like a figure in a stained-glass window, but alas, in actual fact, he is the dullest and most prosaic of beings. He is dead to the unique possibilities of his position; his only interest in what he sells is the profit it brings to him. His abilities, such as they are, are addressed solely to cutting prices and lessening expenses, except, indeed, when they take a sinister turn and explore the dark mysteries of adulteration.

All the old decorative types seem to have disappeared with the mail-coach and the reaping-hook. At most they only linger in quiet countrysides, and there they have exchanged their former robust vigour for a decrepit age; they are only too obviously the survivals of another day. Life now seems greyer and less interesting. We have lost the feeling for spectacular display that makes so much gaiety. It is an age not of the drama, but of the novel; not to the ear and the eye do we appeal, but rather we absorb things by a mental process, and what before was presented visibly on the stage, with all the accompaniments of action and scenery, is now hidden between the two boards of a book.

But though the picturesque human types are vanishing, houses live longer than men, and change with the times less rapidly. The same roof serves as a covering for many generations, and if one were asked what is the most typical thing in England, one would reply at once, the old English cottage.

The most typical, it is also the most homely, and in this lies the reason why it is still so characteristic, for through all changes the home and the family circle have always been the real centre of English life.

And in its style of building it reflects truly the national character. Its plan is simplicity itself, and from this it grows naturally in whatever direction is useful. A wing is thrown out here, a lean-to added behind; the windows are enlarged or built up, as occasion demands; the house takes on almost an organic life, and grows or dwindles with its inmates. Varying slightly in different localities by dint of local custom, or from the use of materials peculiar to the district, old English cottages have yet a common character, thoroughly English; and this, bar the high, bleak lands of Wales and the north, throughout the whole length and breadth of the land.

The mansions of the great, ' the stately homes of England' as they are called, hardly deserve their title. They are not homely enough. They are the show-places of the country, standing aloof with impressive dignity amid their acres of green grass and groves of noble trees, but they seem more like museums or picture-galleries than English homes. On stated days the great gates are thrown open and throngs of visitors pour in, and are led from room to room and down the long corridors, viewing the ancestral portraits to a garrulous accompaniment of parochial history. It is magnificent, no doubt, and we ought to feel the spell of the old feudal grandeur, but it is very wearisome and seems strangely unreal. Did any one ever really live amid all this icy splendour ? Had it always this look of emptiness, or did it once form a living picture ? Anyhow the memory we carry away is of the caretakers living among the half-forgotten ancestors, the shrouded furniture ; and the streams of visitors, blatant or timid, but obviously out of place in either case, passing in and out of the great doors.

After the house the cool, green park is refreshing— one can breathe there after the stuffy atmosphere within ; but just as the other was not home, so is this not quite nature. It is nature drilled and schooled into orderliness and a show of good behaviour. Everything is trim and neat as in a garden. The very trees are groomed as carefully as the horses ; the aged have their joints filled in with cement, their heavy limbs supported by props and chains ; the fallen branches are picked up, and the dead leaves swept away. Only in the storms of winter, or the exuberance of spring and early summer, does nature burst forth irresistibly and break through all bonds ; but these outbursts are decently smoothed over as quickly as possible, their traces are removed, and order and tidiness reign once more.

There is another class of English house, the typical middle-class home. But it is not usually picturesque. At its best it may be an old building, of Elizabeth's time perhaps, or more often one of the stately and formal buildings of Queen Anne and the Georges. And if the furniture too is old, then indeed we have a house that knows real elegance. In favoured localities one may find old-world towns with whole streets of such houses. The ' New Town ' of Edinburgh, for instance, still breathes of the eighteenth century, when Edinburgh was the northern Athens, and the whole city of Bath is redolent of the charm of Jane Austen ; but such cases are few and far between.

The Victorian middle-class house stands as a monument of respectable bad taste, and bad taste is a fault that is aggravated by respectability. The bald horse-hair furniture, slippery as glass except where it is prickly, the pompous wall-papers, the aggressive carpets, all combine to produce a strange lack of comfort or beauty. Let us be thankful that period has passed now, leaving only a few echoes in the coffee-rooms of country hotels, where Gladstone still glares at Beaconsfield smiling his satirical smile on the opposite wall.

We have other ideals now, since the coming of *l'art nouveau*, and the rise of the suburban villa. 'Art in the home' is the cry, and so much art gets in that there is often very little home. Stained glass in the windows, cheap over-ornamented furniture, cheap stamped metal-work, with the hammer marks accurately reproduced by machinery (most people have forgotten that those little dimples are meant to represent hammer marks), ornaments everywhere. Then the pictures ; reproductions of the old masters (as a rule much too small), jostling enlarged photographs (certainly much too large), and the works of the artistic member of the family, all in the cheapest and worst of frames. Then art muslin curtains and a gas-fire. It makes one long for the dulness of the Victorian house, which at least had a sort of after-dinner feeling of repose. The other suggests indigestion and a waking nightmare.

No; if you wish to find the typical English home, you must leave the cities behind you, and go out into the country; you must pass by the mansions of the great and the prosperous homes of the middle classes, and you will find it in the humble cottage.

For it is not the large houses that live in the memory of the visitor. He goes through them as a matter of duty, and forgets about them as a matter of course. The pictures that linger in his mind, called up in a moment by such sensations as the smell of roses or of new-mown hay, are of a simpler nature. A little cottage nestling amidst the wayside trees, the blue smoke curling up against the green, and a bower of roses round the door; or perhaps a village street of which the name has been long forgotten, with its rambling old inn, and, a little distance away, the hoary, grey church-tower in its township of tomb-stones—these are the pictures of old England that are carried away to other climes. And it is the cottage, more homely than the inn, more sacred than the church, that we remember best.

Such places have no history at all, their life has not been set in the public eye, and they have always been so wrapt up in their own affairs, that they have never noticed how time is passing, and so they have brought down into the life of to-day the traditions of two or three hundred years ago.

But though they do not pose, those quiet places, yet it is through them that the deep, main current of English life has flowed. For it is a shallow theory that views history as the annals of a court, or the record of the lives of a few famous men. Doubtless such have their significance, but it is easy to overrate their importance, and they afford but little clue to the life of the people, which is the real history of the country. And until recent days it was not through the cities that this main stream flowed, but through innumerable little country towns and villages.

Washington Irving grasped this fact nearly a hundred years ago when he wrote : ' The stranger who would form a correct opinion of English character must go forth into the country. He must sojourn in villages and hamlets ; he must visit castles, villas, farmhouses, cottages ; he must wander through parks and gardens, along hedges and green lanes ; he must loiter about country churches, attend wakes and fairs and other rural festivals, and cope with the people in all their conditions, and all their habits and humours.'

And these little villages and hamlets are planted all over England, sometimes close together, sometimes more widely spread, but seldom more than a mile or two apart. Written history may have nothing to say regarding them, but they have helped to make history. They have gathered few legends beyond those which time has written on the walls in weather stains and grey lichen, but the men who were born in those humble cottages have wrought in other lands legends that live to-day. Their cosy homes were but newly built when the desperate tides of the civil war surged round them. Half a century later they formed part of the army which 'swore terribly in Flanders,' and in fifty years more they were laying the foundations of our great Indian empire. Then the arid fields of Spain saw them as they followed the Iron Duke through the dogged years of the Peninsular war, and they took part in his crowning triumph at Waterloo. Later still, India knew them once more, and the snowy trenches of the Crimea, and but yesterday Afghanistan, Egypt, and South Africa called them forth again.

And all the while that those truant birds upheld the

name of England abroad, leaving their bones in many lands, their brothers and sisters carried forward the old traditions at home, living their busy, unobtrusive, useful lives, and lying down to rest at last in the old familiar churchyard. And after all, this last is the real life of England, for the sake of which those wars were waged and bloody battles fought. It is the productive life which brings wealth and prosperity and happiness to a nation, and lays the foundation of all that is its honour and its pride.

There is nothing obtrusive about the old cottages. They do not dominate the landscape, but are content to be part of it, and to pass unnoticed unless one looks specially for their homely beauties. The modern house, on the other hand, makes a bid for your notice. It is built on high ground, commands a wide range of country, and is seen from far and wide. But the old cottage prefers to nestle snugly in shady valleys. The trees grow closely about it in an intimate, familiar way, and at a little distance only the wreath of curling smoke tells of its presence.

Indeed the old cottage has always been something so very close and so familiar to us, that its charms have been almost entirely overlooked, and it is only of recent years, when fast falling into decay, that it has formed a theme for pen and pencil. Truth to tell, of late years a change has come over England. The life that the old cottage typifies is now a thing of the past, and is daily fading more and more into the distance. Twentieth-century England, the England of the railway, the telegraph, and the motor-car, is not the England of these old cottages. Our point of view has changed. We no longer see the old homely life from within, but from the outside. But the commonplace of yesterday becomes the poetry of to-day, such a glamour does the magician Time cast over things, and the old life becomes ever more and more attractive as it slips away from us, and we watch it disappear with regretful and kindly eyes.

Architects now find the cottage worth their study, and eminent authorities have written volumes extolling its simple beauties. Formerly it was only the larger buildings, the noblemen's seats and the manor-houses, that were deemed worthy of consideration, but now the same elements of beauty are recognised in the humble forms, and the old cottage is held up as a model to the architectural student.

' The great lesson to be learned from the study of these old examples,' writes Mr. Ralph Nevill, F.S.A., ' is, I take it, the extreme value of simplicity. It is a lesson peculiarly needed, since, even when an architect is willing to work on such lines, it is seldom that his client is content to let him.

'There is more beauty in a cottage of one of the simpler forms . . . with its roof bright with lichen and its front covered with creepers, than we shall ever get from modern examples, tortured as they are into fantastic shapes where all repose and simplicity is lost.

'Anxious, however, as the landowner generally is to secure economy of cost, it is not often that he can be persuaded to trust to simplicity of line and good proportion rather than to overcrowded gables and fantastic barge boards.'

One good result of this change of attitude is the increasing care bestowed on the restoration of these old buildings, though still in too many cases they are ruthlessly destroyed to make room for modern barracks, or improved out of all semblance to their former selves.

Another result, not quite so much to be rejoiced at, is the craze for building the imitation old cottages which are now springing up everywhere.

But the real old cottages had serious faults. Their situation was often unhealthy in the extreme. It seemed as if the old-fashioned Englishman were damp proof, such a leaning towards low-lying ground he displayed. Then again he knew nothing of the convenience of a modern drainage system and carried the water for the household laboriously in pails from the well. He lived so much in the open air that it mattered little to him if his bedroom, with its low windows buried under the eaves, was close and stuffy; and if the kitchen chimney smoked, why, wood smoke was healthy, and one could always open the door.

So in the modern old-fashioned cottage one has the outward semblance of a primitive simplicity, while inside are the latest modern appliances. The roof is thatched, but there is a telephone wire running from it. The kitchen is used for living-room, and we are studiously mediæval in the matter of settles and trestle-tables, but we switch on the electric light when required, and the bath-room is supplied with hot and cold water.

In one respect the old cottages are like old ballads; we have no idea who their authors were. They belong to the countryside, and seem just to have grown there, tinged and coloured by all the local influences of soil and climate. Their architect was the village carpenter, for builder and carpenter were the same, when wood was the chief material employed. Tradition was his school, the methods handed down from father to son were his only methods, but he displayed intelligence and ingenuity in adapting them to the special requirements of the moment. For it is a characteristic of the old life that each little community is complete in itself, solving its own problems without assistance or advice from the outside. It was a narrow and a parochial life perhaps, but it was independent. Often a particular variation of the general style is confined to quite a narrow district, where it is repeated from generation to generation.

But though in ninety-nine cases out of a hundred this veil of anonymity hangs over the authorship of the cottage, yet there is a hundredth case, and we have actually a record of an architect, well known in his time, who, though he earned his reputation by the erection of more pretentious structures, yet was also a builder of simple cottages some of which still exist to-day.

His name was John Abel, and he was born at Hereford in the year 1577. Probably he began as other men did, simply as a carpenter, but by industry and ability so improved his position that he undertook more and more important work. In his prime he was regarded as one of the foremost architects of his day, and he was the builder of many beautiful old timbered structures, the

Town Hall at Leominster, demolished, alas, within the last century, and the Market-Houses of Hereford, Brecknock, and Kingston. Extensive buildings these were ; their elaborate timber frames full of ingenuity and picturesqueness. In Hereford Town Hall were rooms for the fourteen trading companies of the town — Bakers, Barbers, Barber-surgeons, Blacksmiths, Braziers, Butchers, Clothiers, Cordwainers, Glovers, Joiners, Mercers, Tanners, Tylers, and Weavers.

But in addition to these more important works, an unpretentious, though charming little building like the school-house at Weobly, is attributed to him, and must be only one of the many cottages built by him during his long and busy life.

A man of strong individuality and some education, he had a pleasant habit of adorning his work with quaint mottoes and inscriptions. Sometimes those were Latin tags, at other times he used the mother-tongue. In the Town Hall of Leominster, built in 1633, above the columns which supported the upper part of the building one read ' Sat cito si sat bene ' and ' Vive ut post vivans,' and also ' Where justice reigns there virtue flows,' and ' As columns do support the fabric of a building, so noble gentry do subprop the honour of a state.'

More interesting still is the larger inscription in the Market Hall of Kingston (built in 1654, and unfortunately demolished in 1820), which has quite a personal note :

> ' For sellers and buyers this house we prepare,
>   Pray sweare not, nor ly not, in vending your ware ;
>   The world is bad, and when 'twil mend God know,
>   And he that made this house doo help to make it so.'

And again this naïve acknowledgment to the generous donor :

> ' Who build and gave this house if any enquire,
>   A benefactor good to us, called Phillip Holman, Esquire.'

From his deference to rank and authority one would expect Abel in those troublous times to be of the party of the King and not of the Parliament, and this he was, giving proof of his loyalty in a more practical manner, as well as by the engraving of laudatory inscriptions.

He was in Hereford during its siege by the Scotch army in 1645, and took an active part in the defence, rendering such services to the garrison that afterwards Charles conferred on him the position of one of the King's own carpenters. There is something pathetic about this high-sounding dignity conferred so pompously by one who had at the moment lost all the more solid attributes of kingship. But what the Philistine would call barren honours, such as these, are often dearest to the recipient, and we may guess that honest John Abel desired no higher reward for his faithful services.

What those services were is recorded in a despatch by the Governor of the town, Barnabas Scudamore, sent after the raising of the siege to Lord Digby:

'I may not forget one remarkable piece of Divine Providence that God sent us singular men of all professions very useful and necessary to us in this distresse, and so accidentally to us, as if they had been on purpose let down from heaven to save our present and emergent occasions: such as skilful miners, excellent canoneers (one whereof spent but one shot in vain throughout the whole siege), an expert carpenter, the only man in all the country to make mills, without whom we had been much disfurnisht of our means to make powder (after our powder-mill was burnt) or grind corne.

'That Providence that brought these to us at last drove our enemies from us.'

It is noticeable here that Abel, then a man of sixty-eight and at the height of his reputation, builder of such structures as the Town Hall of Leominster, possessing the necessary knowledge to erect such special buildings as mills with all their special requirements, was yet spoken of simply as an expert carpenter.

Abel lived to a ripe old age. He saw the triumph of the Parliamentary party, and then the swing of the pendulum which brought the restoration, and died at last in 1674 at the age of ninety-seven.

When over ninety years of age he seemed to think it time to turn his thoughts to his approaching end, and made his own monument, carving thereon his effigy and that of his two wives, and the symbols of his craft—rule, compass, and square.

Beneath is the following characteristic inscription :

‘ This craggy stone a covering is for an architect's bed,
That lofty buildings raised high, yet now lies down his head ;
This line and rule, so Death concludes, are locked up in store,
Build they who list or they who wist, for he can build no more.
This house of clay could hold no longer,
May Heaven frame him a stronger.’

JOHN ABEL.

CHAPTER II

THE EVOLUTION OF THE COTTAGE—THE EARLY STAGES

'A hut is a palace to a poor man.'
OLD PROVERB.

I HAVE said that one real reason of the directness with which the cottage appeals to us is that, despite its antiquity, it is not too old. Not so old as to be out of touch with our daily life.

Could we see a dwelling of the early Britons absolutely as it was in their days, it would interest us in quite another fashion. We should look at it with the colder gaze of the archæologist, but we should not love it as the home of our fathers, for to us it would hardly appear a home at all. In the world of emotion, which after all is the real world we live in, it would be as remote from us as Stonehenge. One feature of home, indeed, it had, which even now kindles a responsive glow in our hearts, the family hearth, around which English family life begins.

But the old cottage of to-day is not so old that

we need bridge over such a gulf of manners and customs as this. In reality it belongs not to the old life of the Middle Ages, but to the new life which dawned with the coming of the Renaissance to England, and which was the beginning of the modern era. It came when the old institutions of feudalism were finally crumbling away, when the Church ceased to predominate in the civil world, and when the middle classes began for the first time to be a power in the land. The cottage was the home of the sturdy British yeoman. The wars and feuds of earlier times had ceased, trade was increasing, the horizon was expanding, the new world kept pouring treasure into the old, and rural England settled down to a time of peaceful development and prosperity. A calm, sweet, and healthy life, not free from hardships, but carrying with it simple comforts, which lasted unbroken until rudely shaken by the coming of machinery, the new era of steam. And this long period of quiet served England well, for in spite of wars beyond the seas, peace reigned at home save for the few years of the civil war. It was then that the English navy arose, the country waxed rich and prosperous, and our colonies formed outlets to our trades, so that when the new age came, it found us prepared and ready to lead the march of progress, while the rest of the world lagged fifty years at least behind.

One cannot turn back the hands on the dial, but little wonder if, amid the noise and turmoil of modern life, we yearn for the peaceful stillness of earlier days. It is this quiet atmosphere that still haunts the old cottage. It is the symbol of the simple life. Here, it seems to say, is 'rest after toil,' toil simple and healthy under the open sky. And such age as it possesses does not alienate us. It is rendered more venerable, but not less familiar. Doubtless it is an old house ; generation after generation have been born there, have lived their lives there and passed quietly away. Many children have played about the little garden and climbed the gnarled apple-tree ; many an old man has sat on the bench by the door, warming his thin blood in the sunshine, while his grandchildren wake the echoes with their childish laughter. But these were all just men and women like ourselves, thinking our thoughts, speaking our language, the language of the English Bible. If not quite of to-day they are no further off than yesterday.

The quaintness of their old-fashioned ways touches

us more by its half-forgotten familiarity than by any strangeness. It seems to belong to the golden age of our childhood. It makes us feel young again somehow, and we cling to it as we cling to the old authorised version of the Bible, rather than the revised version of to-day. That was the product of the same times as these cottages. It is marked by the same homely strength and beauty, and with age its sanctity has been surrounded with tender associations, just as the grey lichens and green mosses have gathered on the old buildings. The new version is doubtless more correct and more scholarly; the new cottage, it is safe to say, is more sanitary. Yet we cannot build the old cottages now, and we cannot write the English of the old Bible, and so we love and cherish them both. But while the one will live as long as the English language lasts, the days of the other, alas, are numbered. Three hundred years is a long, long life for timber, even old English oak; three hundred years of sun and rain, frost and snow. The old beams feel very old now, and for the cottage in most cases there is only the choice between restoration and speedy decay.

If the restoration is done with a tender hand, the old corner posts, which have rotted below and gradually settled down, carefully raised and underpinned, and the old bent framework to some extent straightened out, perhaps a new lease of life may be given. But the whole building is like an old man twisted with rheumatism; to straighten out the poor old back would be to break it. The most one can do is to prop him up with a couple of sticks to sit in the sun, and beam on us kindly for a few more years.

Though the cottage belongs to an age which is almost modern, yet nowhere is the spirit of conservatism more conspicuous than in architecture, and on examination we shall find in its structure links connecting it with older and more primitive dwellings; curious survivals of days long before the dawn of English history. Indeed its growth is a gradual evolution from these primitive homes of the early Britons.

At the risk of tedium I shall briefly trace this step by step.

The first knowledge we have of the early Britons who inhabited England long before the coming of the Romans, is of a tribal people, subsisting chiefly by hunting, and dwelling in little villages situated along the borders of the woodlands, between their meagre tillage and pasture, and the primeval forest which was their hunting-ground.   But the agricultural clearings were of small extent, and the bulk of the country was covered still with forest and morass, almost impenetrable, or threaded only by a few primitive tracks the secret of which was known to few.   The earliest roads lay along the slopes of the hills, like the famous track which follows the line of the Downs from Winchester to Canterbury, where the steep slope of the ground ensured a dry footing even in the worst weather, and the bare hillside was a guarantee against ambush and surprise.

The homes of these early Britons contained but one room, and under its roof was crowded the whole family, parents, children, and grandchildren.   In plan it was round or square.   A number of upright posts of unhewn or very roughly hewn timber, driven into the ground about a foot apart, the spaces between them being filled in with wattle and daub, formed the walls ; the roof was a wickerwork of interlaced boughs covered with turf.   In the centre of the floor was the family hearth, where the fire was kept burning day and night ; all round the walls were strewn rushes, which served as a seat by day, and which, covered with hides or coarse cloth, formed by night the family couch on which the household lay with their feet towards the fire.

The basis of the whole tribal system thus lay in the family. The right to sit in the family circle and to sleep by the family hearth carried with it the tribesman's right to his share of the common fields and pasture and the tribal hunting-grounds. Such was the British home before the Romans, and many as are the centuries which have passed since then, the term 'the family circle' still survives, and in a modified form the intercourse it stands for is still the basis of English social life. The hearth, too, is still the emblem of domestic comfort. 'Hearth and Home' are words that go naturally linked together.

Near Glastonbury the remains of such a British village has been discovered, dating, so archæologists say, from some 200 B.C.; but primitive though the settlement was, its inhabitants were yet far removed from barbarism. From the specimens found there we know that their weapons and implements were of iron. They used tools; the knife, the spade, the awl, and the bill-hook. The women, too, were busy at home as the men were busy in the hunting-field. They were weavers and spinners, and the weaving combs discovered are numerous and perfect. They made pottery, well decorated and highly finished, and the arts of self-adornment did not lag behind, as the rings of jet, amber, and glass, and bracelets, brooches, and safety-pins of bronze remain to show.

But with the Roman invasion and the period of Roman dominion there comes a strange gap. This long period of years seems but a time of arrested development, a mere digression of four centuries from the main narrative. When the Romans disappear we resume the thread of the tale. They certainly brought a civilisation far in advance of that which existed in the country, but they kept it to themselves. They built walled cities with busy market-places full of trade ; well-made roads connected town with town, and at intervals on these main roads were studded the palatial dwellings of the Roman patricians. Buildings constructed of solid stonework, and spreading often over several acres of ground, of which the tessellated pavements and the fragments of richly decorated walls remain to attest their magnificence, while the sumptuous baths and elaborate arrangements for artificial heating give us some idea of their luxury and comfort. But this higher civilisation of which we have a glimpse never touched the natives of the country. In fact, it must have been reserved for the very few, a select class of officers and higher officials. The great mass of the Roman legionaries were recruited from tribes as barbarous as were the Britons, and once the island was subdued the Britons themselves supplied the soldiers for legions stationed in other countries. The natives of the country sank into the position of slaves to the conquerors, tilling the fields, herding the cattle, tending the horses, and living in their own rude hovels outside the Roman quarters. Indeed the Romans seemed to have been as distinct from the people of England as the English rulers now are from the native population in India. The one class rules, the other obeys, but there is little sympathy and almost no intercourse between them. The iron hand of the ruler enforces law and the equitable administration of justice, and the country prospers; but one can imagine that if the British rule in India were to cease to-morrow, in a few years' time the dark stream of native life would have submerged all its landmarks. A few great bridges and other engineering works rapidly falling into disrepair would linger for a while like the old disused irrigation tanks that now remain as monuments to other and forgotten rulers.

This was what happened in England when the Romans, harassed by the inroads of the barbarian at home, finally abandoned Britain; they left behind a people but little touched by their civilisation. But the islanders were not allowed to remain in undisturbed possession, for as the Romans went, their place was taken by hordes of warlike tribes from the mainland, Angles, Jutes, and Saxons.

All through the fifth and sixth centuries these invaders came pouring in; their feeble defences were swept away, and the native Britons found that in getting rid of the Romans they had only exchanged one set of masters for another.

The new masters, however, were of a different type from the old. A rude and vigorous race, they lived almost entirely in the open air and held in contempt the costly palaces and rich cities of the Romans. They burnt the towns and razed the villas to the ground, for it was their custom not to allow a single building of their enemies to stand. For them a stout timber-built hall with a few outhouses was a sufficient habitation, a moat and a stockade a strong fortification; as for the British serfs and bondsmen, their miserable wattled cots sufficed for them.

So the influence of Rome passed away as though

it had never been. Its most permanent results were the great roads, driven through swamps and forest, over mountain and moor, which spanned the country from end to end and endure to this day, and also the improved methods of agriculture which the British serfs carried on for the benefit of their new masters. Perhaps too in the towns Roman buildings still survived to some extent, and are the originals of such curious anomalies as the rows in Chester.

In the province of domestic architecture, which is our main interest, we may count the Roman influence as nil; the walled cities and elaborate stone villas perished absolutely, leaving no trace of their presence in the work of succeeding generations of builders. They never affected the style of the dwellings of the people.

The Anglo-Saxons brought their own manners and customs with them, and though doubtless mingling to some extent with the original inhabitants—for the presence of many words of Celtic origin attest to the survival of the Celtic element—yet they were the dominant race, and under their rule the social order arose which has existed with but little modification until modern times.

As a dweller in well-wooded districts, the Anglo-

Saxon built in wood; indeed in his language the word to build, 'timbran,' signified to build with wood, and builder meant carpenter. In course of time, after many feuds, the local tribes gradually amalgamated, uniting under more or less powerful leaders; and as the country grew in prosperity, it is safe to assume that the wooden buildings of the people were of more solid materials and of greater size than those of the earlier Celtic inhabitants—in fact, that the old English timber-built house dates from before the Conquest, and has its origin in these rude halls of the Anglo-Saxons.

What these were we can only judge of from the most primitive examples yet remaining. The oldest form of rectangular house was erected in 'bays,' the simplest form of construction being the house of one 'bay.' Two pairs of bent trees were set up in the ground about sixteen feet apart, each pair forming a Gothic arch, and united at their apexes by a beam forming a ridge-tree. This framework was then strengthened by two tie-beams, making each arch into a large letter A, and was fastened together with large wooden pegs.

The space between the two arches or 'gavels' (hence gable) was sixteen feet, the space required for the housing of one team of oxen as they stood in the yoke, and this measure of a ' bay ' became an architectural unit ; as late as the beginning of the seventeenth century a house being talked of as ' of so many bays.' This origin of the ' bay ' would seem to show that at first the oxen were stalled under the same roof as sheltered the family, an arrangement which still obtains in the wilder parts of the Hebrides, where cattle, poultry, and crofters all live huddled in one miserable room, without light and without ventilation.

The oldest of these buildings had no upper story, and the walls were made of wattle-work plastered with clay or mud, the roofs probably of thatch. In the earliest form the walls and roof were made in one continuous slope, in fact the building was like an inverted boat ; the next step was to make the walls straight, and thus largely to increase the roomi-ness of the interior. The method was, to produce the ends of the tie-beam (the cross-bar of the letter A) till it became equal in length to the base of the gable arch. On the ends of the tie-beams thus extended, long beams known as ' pons ' or ' pans ' were placed, and then the rafters laid between the ' pans ' and ridge-tree. The walls were built up from the ground till the ' pan ' rested on the top of the wall. The

PLATE 1. AN ANCIENT COTTAGE, I.W.

PLATE 2. COTTAGE NEAR FRESHWATER, I.W.

PLATE 3. COTTAGE NEAR TORQUAY

PLATE 4. SANDHILLS, WITLEY, SURREY

PLATE 5. COTTAGE NEAR OXFORD

PLATE 6. A HAMPSHIRE COTTAGE

PLATE 7. COTTAGE CHILDREN

PLATE 8. AT DENHAM, BUCKS.

inner supporting framework of gavels was thus enclosed in an outer shell.

This old form still survives, and may be seen even in buildings existing at the present day, an instance of how a traditional form is repeated and repeated even after the necessity for it has passed away. In the plate facing page 84 may be seen an excellent example.[1]

This is the real germ of the old English timber house which in more or less elaborate forms has existed till the present day.

But it is almost impossible to trace the gradual growth of the cottage form. Naturally it was the least permanent of all buildings, and the first to fall into decay or to be pulled down to make way for other structures. Of domestic architecture of an earlier date than the fifteenth century there is very little remaining except the stone castles and manor-houses of the nobility, or perhaps the almshouses and other such buildings found in the old towns. Where a timbered structure does exist of the fifteenth century or earlier, almost invariably (though perhaps used now as a cottage) it was built as something more pretentious. The tracing of the evolution of the cottage, then, resolves itself into

1. Plate 18 in this edition

following the gradual social progress of the people, and gleaning here and there a scrap of information regarding their domestic life.

In Anglo-Saxon times the population of the village consisted of the following classes.

First come the gentry, the thane or landlord living on his own land, but owing special duties of service to the King. The priest, also of gentle blood, living on the glebe with which his patron lord has endowed the village church, receiving and distributing tithes and other church dues. The church, it may be mentioned, was, before the Conquest, in most cases a building not of stone but of wood.

Then we have the second class. These were the farmers or yeomen, freemen, either working their own land or holding it from the landlord. In the latter case they paid him partly in rent and partly in services rendered to him in cultivating his own demesne. The third class were the village tradespeople and artificers, also freemen; they comprised crafts-men of all sorts, pedlars and other traders, hunters, fowlers, and fishers. All the above were probably of Saxon descent.

Then we have the peasants and cottagers, not free-men, and mostly of British descent, working on the lord's land, and receiving in lieu of wages a piece of land to work on their own behalf.

Lowest in the scale came the labourers, mere serfs, paid partly in food and clothing, or in the case of village officials, sometimes dues and other perquisites.

The famous colloquy of Ælfric, a Latin MS. of the beginning of the eleventh century, a copy of which may be seen in the British Museum, gives a vivid picture of the social life of the Anglo-Saxon period. The various characters speak and describe their daily occupations.

The ploughman says: 'I work hard. I go out at daybreak, driving the oxen to the field, and I yoke them to the plough. Be it never so stark winter I dare not linger at home for awe of my lord; but having yoked my oxen and fastened share and coulter, every day I must plough a full acre or more. I have a boy driving the oxen with a goad iron, who is hoarse with cold and shouting. And I do more also. I have to fill the oxen's binns with hay and water and take out their litter. Mighty hard work it is, for I am not free.'

The shepherd: 'In the first of the morning I drive my sheep to their pasture and stand over them in heat and in cold with my dogs, lest the wolves swallow them up, and I lead them back to their folds and milk them twice a day, and their folds I move, and I make cheese and butter, and I am true to my lord.'

The oxherd: 'When the ploughman unyokes the oxen I lead them to pasture, and all night I stand over them waking against thieves, and then in the early morning I betake them, well filled and watered, to the ploughman.'

The King's hunter: 'I braid me nets and set them up in fit places and set my hounds to follow up the wild game till they come unsuspectingly to the net and are caught therein and I slay them in the net. With swift hounds I hunt down wild game. I take harts and boars and bucks and roes and sometimes hares. I give the King what I take because I am his hunter. He clothes me well and feeds me, and sometimes gives me a horse or an arm ring that I may pursue my craft the more merrily.'

The fisher says: 'I go on board my boat and cast my net in the river, and cast my angle and baits, and what they catch I take. The citizens buy my fish, but I cannot catch as many as I could sell.' In the river he gets 'eels and pike, minnows and eelpout, trout, and lamphreys,' and in the sea 'herring and salmon, porpoises and sturgeon, oysters and crabs and mussels, periwinkles, sea-cockles, plaice and fluke and lobsters and many of the like,' but he seldom fishes in the sea, 'for it is a far row for me to the sea.' 'It is a perilous thing to catch a whale. It is pleasanter for me to go to the river with my boat than to go with many boats whale-hunting.'

The fowler: 'In many ways I tricke the birds, sometimes with nets and gins with lime, with whistling, with a hawk, with traps. The hawks feed themselves and me in winter, and in Lent I let them fly off to the woods, and I catch the young birds in harvest and tame them. But many feed the tamed ones the summer over, that they may have them ready again.'

The merchant: 'I go aboard my ship with my goods and go over sea and sell my things, and buy precious things which are not produced in this country, and bring them hither. And I sell them dearer here than I buy them there, that I may get some profit wherewith I may feed myself and my wife and sons.'

Such was England before the Norman Conquest. The body-servants, and indeed the bulk of the agricultural labourers, lived in the hall of their thane or landlord. The freemen probably occupied their own rude huts, but they were comparatively few in number.

The Saxon hall was a timber building, probably roofed with shingles or thatch, and surrounded by a stockaded moat. Stone was not used then to any great extent. Even the churches of Saxon times were, as a rule, of wood, and the great stone castles, the ruins of which cover England, belong to a later date. In the Domesday Book survey, Arundel is the only castle mentioned as existing in the time of Edward the Confessor. There seems, however, to have been a tendency for the hall to become more and more important, and for the labourers to come more and more under the dominion of the lord of the manor, until the old free ' ceorl ' had become the ' villein ' known to Norman lawyers. But till after the Conquest there was no sharp distinction between class and class, such as came with the rise of feudalism, when the dominant factor in the division of ranks was the possession of land, determining, with an automatic precision, each man's position in the social scale.

Such cottagers' dwellings as existed in those days must have been of the most primitive description, little advanced from the wattled structures formed of undressed timber and interlaced boughs of the early Britons.

But though, as regards domestic comfort, comparatively little progress had been made, yet gradually a stable social system was being established, differing in its essentials but little from that which exists to-day.

And so another period of three or four hundred years goes by. Then comes the last great invasion of England, the Norman Conquest. Apart from the scenes of bloodshed and desolation which accompanied the actual conquest, this appears in the main to have been wonderfully humane in its actions, and in the end largely for the public good. The powerful hand of the Norman kings welded the country together into one homogeneous whole as it had never been before, and the Normans soon ceased to be Normans and became English. In fact, here we must give up one of the most cherished beliefs of our childhood. The conflict of Norman and Saxon so vividly portrayed in Scott's *Ivanhoe*, and echoed in Macaulay's pages, seems to have had little foundation in fact. In a wonderfully short time Saxon and Norman had become one nation.

The famous Domesday Book survey made by

William the Conqueror in 1086 gives a valuable account of the state of the country. Five million acres were then under tillage, employing a population of some two million, burgesses, clergy, and artificers not being included in this number.

Of these 1400 were tenants in chief and 7900 under-tenants, all these ranking as gentry. Then come the freeholders, 12,000, and the yeomen, 23,000 in number, all of whom would live in their own houses. Thirdly come the villein or copyholders (so called because the sole title to their lands consisted of an extract copied from the rent-roll of the manor), and 90,000 small copyholders (cottars and bordars), who, unless living in the hall of the lord of the manor, must have inhabited the merest hovels.

The average holding of a villein seemed to be about thirty acres, in return for which he had to pay a small rent, plough four acres for the lord of the manor, supply two oxen for the common plough team, and perform other duties. The cottar held, as a rule, five acres (though in later surveys the amount sometimes rises to twelve acres), and for this he had to render to his lord one day's work per week, besides paying for the use of pasture. The lord of the manor usually farmed his own land through a bailiff.

But these various holdings did not form a series of compact farms, each one standing by itself, as we should now expect. The ground was farmed in common, and the land of the typical village was divided into four divisions. One part wheat, one barley, or oats, one lying fallow, and the rest pasture. Each field was roughly marked out by bands of turf into narrow strips representing the different holdings, of which one in every five might belong to the lord, one in every ten to the Church, and so on. The fields were ploughed, harrowed, sown and reaped by the joint labour of all the holders. Each contributed his quota of labour and of stock according to re-cognised custom. A cumbrous and wasteful method it seems in many ways, for a villein's holding of thirty acres might consist of thirty or forty different strips scattered all over the parish ; but economical in this way, that implements and stock were used in common, and the expense thus distributed over the whole, a system almost necessary in the case of such small holdings.

CHAPTER III

THE EVOLUTION OF THE COTTAGE (*continued*)

'An Englishman's house is his castle.'

OLD PROVERB.

THE Norman Conquest brought a great change in the architecture of the country. From Normandy came the great church-builders, and soon, in place of the old wooden structures, noble edifices of stone reared their massive towers above the surrounding plain. The Norman nobles, too, among whom the conquered territory was apportioned, built themselves huge castles of solid stone, for the art of war was becoming more complex, and the old stockades and moats that were a sufficient defence for the Saxon halls, would have been but a slight protection against the more heavily armed and better equipped armies of Norman times.

For the most part now, and for many years later, the use of stone was restricted to these more important buildings. The manor-house of the gentry and the huts of the people were built of wood, and were only a development of the older Saxon dwellings.

The halls, however, were much more pretentious structures than the old Saxon dwellings, for especially in the early years of Norman rule, the King and his barons maintained a large force of foreign mercenaries. The elastic Saxon regime was exchanged for the rigid rule of feudalism, partaking more of the nature of a military organisation, and during the first two hundred years of Norman dominion, the old Saxon freemen tended more and more to become the mere chattels of the lord of the manor. Their cots were little better than hovels. Four walls plastered over with mud, and roofed with boughs, or a thatch of straw, they differed but little from the rude huts of the earliest times. The interior was almost destitute of furniture, save for a rude trestle-table, a bench or two, and a bed of straw.

It is through the manor-house that we must trace the evolution of domestic architecture. Afterwards, in more prosperous times, the improvements which it had undergone were adapted to the cottages of the people, for the same builders built both the hall and the cottage.

The home of the Norman baron, whether of stone

or wood, had one essential feature, the spacious and lofty hall, going right up to the roof, which was the centre of the social life of the day. In the middle of the floor stood the open hearth, the smoke finding its way out through a hole in the roof. At one end was a vaulted cellar, above which was the retiring room for the lord's family, the ' solar ' it was called, or room in which to take the sun. Other buildings, kitchen, pantry, buttery, and so forth, were added as required ; but the hall itself was the common dining-room and the sleeping-apartment of retainers and humbler visitors. Rushes were strewn on the floor of the hall, though the solar sometimes had a carpet. But these huge apartments, rude though they were, were often decorated with great magnificence. Stained glass filled the windows (the window-frames were often portable, so that they could be carried from house to house), fresco-paintings and costly tapestries covered the walls.

A fine example of the old baronial hall, dating from early Norman times, may be seen, still in a state of almost perfect preservation, at Penshurst Place, near Tonbridge. The raised dais at one end, where the lord of the manor and his friends sat at a separate table, the hearth in the centre of the floor, the huge oaken tables resting on trestles, are still there. At one end is a gallery for musicians, and in the wall above is a little loophole through which the lord, seated at ease in the solar, might still keep an eye on the retainers below.

But as time went on the whole system of life began to change. The feudal tie ceased to bind so closely, the nobles gradually declined in power, while the common people began to assume a new importance. The change was felt first in the towns, trade and craft guilds were formed, and the burghers bit by bit won from their overlords, usually by actual purchase, the right to manage their own affairs. In the country the change came more slowly, for the yeomen had not either the growing wealth of the burghers, or the strength that comes from numbers or organisation. Gradually, however, a change came about in the relations between them and the lord of the manor. Formerly the latter had cultivated his own demesne through a bailiff, being entitled to services in labour from the villeins, but now he found it to his advantage to let the land to them, exacting a rent payable in money or in kind. The usual word for the rent was 'feorm,' from which we have the word farm, and the rise of the farmer marks the beginning of the decay of the feudal system. A class of men arose, independent, sturdy, and respectable, who soon made their presence felt. It was the English yeomen who at Crecy changed the whole system of warfare, and made the bowman more dreaded than the knight-at-arms, but their influence at home was even more important and far-reaching. The changed relations also spread to the lower class of agricultural labourers. From being mere serfs, these gradually rose to the position of labourers, receiving daily wages, and free to work for whom they chose. By the end of the first half of the fourteenth century, landlords, as a general rule, paid a pound an acre for the cultivation of their land.

Material conditions had also changed very much for the better. Langland the poet, writing a few years after 1350, says: 'Labourers that have no land to live on but their hands, disdained to live on penny ale or bacon, but demanded fresh flesh or fish, fried or baked, and that hot and hotter for chilling of their maw, and but if they be highly hired; else will they chide and wail the time that they were made workmen.' Indeed, in physical well-being, probably the agricultural labourer was better off than he has been at any subsequent time.

The houses of the better-class yeomen now began for the first time to approximate to the cottage type known to us to-day. They were timber houses, built on a frame, as in later times, and filled in with wattle and daub or clay. The floor was bare earth, and the sleeping-apartment under the thatch was reached by a ladder or a rude staircase. A few chests ranged round the walls; a rude table and benches formed the furniture. The bacon rack was fastened to the timbers overhead, and the walls of the homestead were garnished with agricultural implements. The wood-fire stood on a hearth of clay, chimneys were unknown except in castles or manor-houses, and the smoke escaped by the door, or through any other aperture it could find. Artificial light was too costly for general use. When it got dark the inmates sat over the fire or went to bed. The dunghill stood just outside the door.

Rude as it is, such a dwelling marks a great advance in comfort, and may be termed the first English Cottage, and would indeed compare well with the cabins of the Irish peasantry, or the homes of the West Highland crofters of the present day.

All over the country was the same increase of prosperity The towns were thriving and wealthy, the burghers many of them men of substance, living in houses more luxuriously furnished than those of the country farmers. The trade of the country was growing rapidly. Never had prospects seemed more rosy than in the early years of the fourteenth century. It seemed as though the dark times of the Middle Ages were over and a new era of rapid progress had been inaugurated, when there occurred suddenly a catastrophe, peculiarly characteristic, which for at least two hundred years delayed this peaceful and silent evolution. In 1348 the terrible epidemic known as the Black Death visited the country and swept it from end to end. Of the three or four millions which formed the population of England, more than half died in the repeated visitations of this awful scourge. Its ravages were fiercest in the large towns, where the insanitary conditions aggravated the evil, but the country villages suffered almost as heavily. Norwich was reduced to a third of its population, and from the second city of the country dropped to the position of the sixth. The wealthy suffered with the poor, and the Church perhaps suffered most heavily of all. In Yorkshire more than one-half of the priesthood is said to have perished.

For a time the ordinary work of agriculture became almost impossible. ' The sheep and cattle strayed through the fields and corn, and there were none left who could drive them,' writes a contemporary. The fields were left untilled, the harvests rotted on the ground, the whole organisation of labour was thrown out of gear. Manorial records here in many cases show a suggestive gap ; the tenants, and probably also the recorder, had all been swept away.

The effects of this terrible mortality were manifold. In the first place, the amount of available labour was decreased by about half. But in addition to this, in many cases whole families of tenant-farmers had been carried off, and their lands had reverted to the lord of the manor, who found himself at one and the same time deprived of his rents and forced either to let the land go out of cultivation or to hire labour to work it.

But with the greatly reduced supply of labour, and the largely increased demand for it, the inevitable happened ; the labourers were masters of the situation, and put up their prices, refusing to work at the old low rates, which indeed, with the greatly increased prices of corn and other necessaries, would hardly have sufficed to support them. Nowadays we consider their behaviour only natural, and are

apt to look upon the action of the landlords, in
endeavouring to re-enforce the old rates, as mere
oppression; but, after all, there is much to be said on
either side. The landlords were in a difficult position,
with their land lying idle on their hands, and their
rent-roll reduced perhaps by one-half. It must be
remembered, too, that the modern principle of competition in fixing the price of labour was then something quite unheard of. In resisting the increased
demands of the peasantry, the landlord felt that he
had right on his side, and he certainly had law.
For the gradual emancipation of the villein from his
feudal services had been largely a matter of custom,
arising from mutual advantage, but never placed on
a legal footing. The old feudal statutes had never
been repealed, and the landlords would have been
something more than human if they had not taken
advantage of their legal position, and tried to
enforce the old conditions of servitude. But they
did more. As the strife became more bitter, new laws
were passed forbidding wages to rise above a certain
height; and to defeat those who thought by a change
of district to at once escape their feudal obligations,
and find a remunerative market for their labour,
labourers were forbidden to travel.

Another thing happened which rendered the conflict more bitter than ever. Sheep-farming was coming more and more into vogue. The excellence of English wool was causing an increased demand for it abroad, and its price rose rapidly. It is not to be wondered at that here the landlord saw a way out of his difficulties, and wherever possible placed his whole demesne under pasture. His profits increased, for wool fetched a high price, and his expenses were greatly reduced, as one or two shepherds now took the place of numerous agricultural labourers. But it had dire consequences to the labourer. As the arable land changed to pasture, he saw his livelihood disappear, often his cottage was pulled down and he and his family turned adrift, and the countryside, which a few years before had supported a busy agricultural community, was now unpopulated save for a few lonely shepherds.

Enclosing, as it was popularly termed, carried with it another danger which was to become more and more evident as time went on, in the temptation it offered the landlord to absorb the land of his weaker neighbours. Sometimes a fair compensation was paid, sometimes the land was seized by force, often it was obtained by fraud ; and by all these methods the large estates grew larger and the smallest holdings tended to disappear.

Fortunately, another method adopted by the land-lords did something to mitigate this evil, and was entirely good in its effects. This was the system of leasing land to the more substantial free labourers, which more than any other cause tended to raise the status of this sturdy agricultural class. As such tenants were, of course, poor men, the agreement was what was termed a 'stock and land lease,' and under it the landlord not only leased the land to the tenant, but lent the stock and implements required to cultivate it. These or their equivalent were returned to the landlord on the expiry of the term. The method worked well, for the free labourers, tempted by the idea of becoming their own masters, were thus induced to pay a reasonable rent to the landlord, instead of his having to employ them at high wages to farm the land for him with doubtful results. So rapid was their prosperity that in many cases land held by the farmer on short term stock and land leases, had in little more than a generation paid off all obligations to the landlord, and were held under ordinary long term leases.

These two methods then, leasing and sheep-farming, went hand in hand on the best managed estates. The Church especially, which owned a great part of the land of the country, leased largely to yeomen, and though scrupulously exacting its dues, was a lenient and kindly landlord.

Both methods pressed hardly on the poorest classes, for the leases only went to the best of the labouring population, and land continued to go out of cultivation. Discontent grew more and more widespread, especially as the restrictive legislation regarding the payment of labour continued, and the general misery and discontent culminated in the famous peasants' rising of 1381. John Ball, the priest of Kent, was its most popular leader. His followers carried a banner with the rude couplet

> ' When Adam delved and Eve span,
> Who was then the gentleman ? '

and communism was his cure for social evils. It was the first note in the war between labour and capital, which is growing louder and louder in modern times.

But the insurrection failed; the old laws were re-enacted with such stringency, that in many parts of the country villeinage still lingered in Queen Elizabeth's reign. The fourteenth century then

closed with a period of reaction, the promise of its
beginning cruelly belied ; and the new century began
with injustice and oppression.

The fifteenth century is a period about which it
is difficult to get accurate information. In spite,
however, of such features as the oppression of the
agricultural labourers, and the cruel War of the Roses,
the years went on with a steady advance in the
national well-being. And the domestic architecture
of the day reflected this advance in general comfort.
The manor-house increased in size, the hall ceased
to be the common sleeping- and living-room of the
household, new rooms were added. The dais was
portioned off, and formed a dining-room or parlour.
Separate bedrooms followed, and, curious mark of
growing refinement, at this time the use of night-
shirts became general. The old lofty hall in most
cases ceased to exist, often a floor cut it in half, the
upper part forming bedrooms, the lower part living-
rooms, and in many existing old houses it is found
in this condition.

With the greater comfort of the manor-house came
an improvement in the position of the lower classes.
There was a constant increase in the yeomen tenant-
farmer class, many of whom attained a position of

solid well-being, and were able, not only to maintain their families, but often so to educate them, as to fit them, in their turn, for still higher positions.

Bishop Latimer, preaching before Edward VI., draws a picture, contrasting the prosperity of the fifteenth-century farmer with the evil case of his successor in the sixteenth century, and gives a fine portrait of a typical yeoman.

' My father,' says he, ' was a yeoman, and had no lands of his own ; only he had a farm of three or four pounds by the year, at the uttermost, and here-upon he tilled so much as kept half-a-dozen men. He had walk for one hundred sheep, and my mother milked thirty kine. He was able, and did find the King a harness, with himself and horse. He kept me to school, and my sisters he married with five pounds apiece. He kept hospitality for his poor neighbours, and some alms he gave to the poor, and all this he did of the same farm.'

The cottages of these yeomen, too, began to be dotted about the countryside, and now we at last get in touch with modern times, for some of these fifteenth-century cottages still survive, though, as a rule, greatly added to and altered. They are of the familiar, half-timbered style, and are marked by a certain primitive simplicity. The chimney, if there is any, is a later addition, and is usually built on outside the house. The timber work has the panels close together, as is the case in early sixteenth-century cottages also, and as a rule the first-floor projects slightly over the ground-floor, leaving the ends of the rafters visible. Most of the fifteenth-century buildings, however, now used as cottages, were not built as such, but have come down in the world, having once belonged to wealthier and more pretentious people.

In the towns, too, wealth was increasing. In addition to the merchant and shopkeeper class had arisen a class of independent craftsmen, who earned from fourpence three-farthings to sixpence a day, equal in our money to about twenty or thirty shillings a week, an income on which they could live comfortably and yet lay by. Their houses were superior to the country cottage in style and comfort, and examples of them may still be seen in such old towns as Shrewsbury and Tewkesbury. An excellent example of the fifteenth-century building may be seen in the plate facing page 154[1]. Situated in West Tarring, near Worthing, this is noted as one of the best remaining examples of the period. Particularly

1. Plate 35 in this edition

fine is the cusped and traceried barge-board, so much more labour expended upon it than in later days, when there was a greater demand on the builder's time. The other marks of an early date are there too, the overhanging upper story, supported on a huge beam, and the narrow spacing of the posts. All the requisites for cottage building were now at hand. The increased standard of comfort demanded them, and there was no lack of competent workmen to build them. Whenever the yeomen could afford it, the cottage was there, but the country still had to wait nearly a hundred years before it became the usual dwelling of the people.

What was wanted was simply more money to spend.

But changes were going on which prepared the country for the wave of prosperity when it did come. Commerce was growing, and the commercial spirit was rapidly replacing the old ideas of feudalism. It is a significant fact that the Commons were now beginning to assume a leading position in Parliament. Formerly a distinction had been drawn between borough and county members. The first, drawn from the merchant classes, were regarded as authorities on questions of finance, but had little or no voice in matters of state, but this distinction was swept away, and the citizen members and the knights of the shire discussed such questions on an equality. England, indeed, had ceased to be purely an agricultural country, and commerce was becoming daily more important. With the increase of trade and the growing prosperity of the larger yeomen farmers, there arose a new force in the country, the middle class.

But the agricultural depression continued still. Sheep-farming increased by leaps and bounds, the proportion of arable land decreased, till the lot of the peasantry was miserable indeed. Sir Thomas More regards this as the crying evil of his time, and calls on us to sympathise with the 'husbandmen thrust out of their own, or else by covin or fraud or by violent oppression put beside it, or by wrongs and injuries so wearied that they sell all'; and he goes on to denounce 'the noblemen and gentlemen, yea and certain abbots, that lease no ground for tillage, that enclose all into pasture and pull down houses; that pluck down towns and leave nothing standing, but only the church to be made a sheep-house.'

When the sixteenth century dawned the time was ripe for changes. And of these the most far-reaching were those which concerned the Church. It is difficult to overrate the importance of the part played by the Church during the Middle Ages. The great monastic houses were the centres of culture and learning, and formed peaceful shelters in times full of strife and violence. But they were more than this, for they acted as the inns of the traveller, and their charities were generous and wide. In practical affairs they were as important, for, next to the crown, they were the greatest landowners in the country; the Church lands afforded employment to vast numbers of agricultural labourers, and at one time they had been the leaders in matters of agriculture.

Now with the new commercial ideas in the air the Church became a conservative force, rather a hinderance than a help to progress. Many of the monasteries had fallen into corruption and decay; some were wellnigh bankrupt.

Then like a crash came their dissolution by Henry VIII. Certainly the motives of those concerned were far from disinterested, but there is little doubt that on the whole the change was for the public good. The new owners were a class of progressive men, anxious to make the most out of their new investment, and little bound by old associations and traditions.

At first, indeed, the change seemed to do little to alleviate the burdens of the agricultural class. In some ways matters seemed to grow worse, for sheep-farming increased to such an extent that the Government was forced to interfere. Laws were passed providing that all land under cultivation must remain in that state, and that no one should own more than two thousand sheep; but these were of little effect, for the very men who had the carrying out of the laws were those who were profiting by the abuses they forbade. So the Acts were easily evaded, sheep were passed off as the property of servants and children, pasture-land had a furrow run through it, and was said to be ploughed.

Another cause kept back the prosperity which seemed gradually to be forcing itself on the country in spite of adverse circumstances. This was the debasement of the coinage by Henry VIII., which unsettled the growing trade of the country to such an extent, that it did not recover for about twenty years. A shilling-piece in 1551 contained only one-seventh of the silver which it contained in 1527. Prices rose enormously, and so distrustful did the people become of the coinage that trade largely degenerated into a system of barter.

But it was as if nothing could restrain the rising tide of England's wealth. The country undoubtedly was thriving. At the death of Henry VIII. in 1547 the population had increased to four millions from two and a half millions in 1485, for the first time regaining the figures at which it stood before the ravages of the Black Death. All that was wanted was peace abroad and good government at home, and these came with the reign of good Queen Bess, from which we date the beginning of modern England.

And in this glorious burst of vitality which marks the Elizabethan age comes the feature which here interests us specially, the great rush of building, which not only reared stately palaces for the nobility and beautiful country-houses for the gentry, but studded every countryside with the homes of the people; and unpretentious as they were, these last may vie with any other buildings in the country for simple, well-ordered beauty, as they surpass them in homeliness and comfort.

CHAPTER IV

THE GREAT BUILDING TIME

'Building is a sweet impoverishing.'
OLD PROVERB.

THE reign of Queen Elizabeth, in which commenced the great building time when the bulk of the old English cottages came into existence, is perhaps the most wonderful period in all English history.

From a dim twilight we suddenly seem to step into bright sunshine. In every department of life there is an astonishing outburst of vigour. The fruits which have been slowly ripening for centuries seem suddenly to come to maturity. England is awake after the slumbers of the Middle Ages, and for a brief period the national life blazes with an unprecedented brilliance and splendour. Too brilliant it is, indeed, to be long sustained, but such as has never since been equalled. And when the extraordinary outburst dies down, it is succeeded by a steady glow of prosperity, which has been maintained with increasing strength until the present day.

A number of circumstances combined to give the age its unique character. In the first place, there sat on the throne a sovereign, who, whatever her personal faults might be, kept this great aim before her, to foster in every way the well-being of her subjects. In the words of the historian Green, 'her love of peace, her instinct of order, the firmness and moderation of her government, the judicious spirit of conciliation and compromise among warring factions, gave the country an unexampled tranquillity at a time when almost every other country in Europe was torn with civil war.' And no sovereign was ever more beloved by her people.

She succeeded to a heritage of confusion and disorder, but with characteristic energy tackled the domestic problems before her without loss of time. One of her first acts was to appoint a commission to inquire into the causes of the widespread social discontent, and the result of its report was the passing of a series of Poor Laws which did much to allay distress, especially in the country districts, and have been in active operation down almost to the present day. By the year 1560 also the debasement of the coinage, which had so dislocated trade, was brought to an end, and trade and commerce thus placed on a sure foundation.

These domestic reforms, however, though they cleared the way and rendered progress easy, did not supply the motive-power. That came from a great wave of life which arose in the nation itself. It seemed as though the race had suddenly shaken off the effects of the pestilence which for two centuries had at intervals wasted England, and had risen up refreshed and invigorated. And there was abundant stimulus from the outside. It was an age when new avenues of thought and action were opening everywhere. The new tide of learning that swept in from Italy was welcomed eagerly. Every gentleman was a scholar, every courtier a poet.

Even the commercial enterprises of the day took on the colours of romance. Men had seen the world expand to twice its former size before their startled eyes. Eldorado was not a vague dream to them, but a reality. They saw ships sail from the little Devon seaports out into the unknown, and return laden deep with silver and gold, and the mariners were full of strange tales of new lands, wilder than any flights of fancy.

And everywhere, to whatever fields of activity we turn, we find the same overflowing vigour. Great men were appearing everywhere. In Lord Bacon we have our first great man of science. In poetry,

PLATE 9. SANDHILLS, WITLEY, (MASTER HARDY'S)

PLATE 10. THE OLD TUCKING MILL, BRIDPORT, DORSET

PLATE 11. AT CHARLTON KINGS, GLOS.

PLATE 12. AT A COTTAGE DOOR, I.W.

PLATE 13. AT BRAEMORE, HANTS.

PLATE 14. 'AFTER FOUR CENTURIES'

PLATE 15. WAXWELL FARM, PINNER

PLATE 16. UNDER HINDHEAD, SURREY

Spenser, though the greatest, is but one of a grove of sweet singers, and these in their turn are wellnigh eclipsed by Shakespeare and his companion giants of the Elizabethan drama. In Drake we have the first of our line of English admirals, and in Sir Walter Raleigh, perhaps the most dazzling figure of his time, the prince of gentleman adventurers.

It was a lavish life; everything seemed to be full to overflowing. The old sobriety of English dress disappeared, and men and women were attired gorgeously and in the brightest colours. The Queen led the way; her wardrobe was magnificent beyond description, and her jewellery was worth a fabulous sum. The old ideas of value seemed to have changed. The young gallants of the Court wore the price of a manor on their backs. Men gambled away a fortune at a sitting, and sailed away to the Spanish main to find another.

Old Chapman well expresses the spirit of adventure and enthusiasm which was abroad when he sings:

> ' Give me a spirit that on this life's rough sea
> Loves to have his sails filled with a lusty wind
> Even till his sail-yards tremble, his masts crack,
> And his wrapt ship turn on her side so low
> That she drinks water and her keel ploughs air.
> There is no danger to a man that knows
> What life and death is.'

Among the common people, too, life seems to have gone bravely and merrily, ' with a hey nonny-nonny.' Every village had its maypole, and the joyous village life has left us a heritage of song surely the sweetest to which shepherd ever tuned his pipe. It seems as if there could have been no grey skies in Elizabeth's England, no dull November days, nothing but a perpetual Mayday, with bursting blossoms, glorious sunshine, and fresh, fair winds.

But if the motive-power sprang from the people themselves, the fuel that fed the flames came from the new prosperity of the country. In 1492, the year of the discovery of America, there had been only thirty millions of coined money in Europe. By the middle of the sixteenth century this amount had risen to about fifty millions, and during the next fifty years silver to the extent of a hundred millions flowed in from the mines of Mexico and Peru. Spain it was that reaped the first direct benefits of this influx, but every year more of it found its way to England. English trade increased everywhere. Sir Thomas Gresham in 1566 founded the Royal Exchange in London, and on the fall of Antwerp in 1584, London took its place as the great mart of the world. English ships sailed the Mediterranean and the Baltic ; they took part in the cod-fishings of Newfoundland and the whale-fishings of the Polar seas. The coast of Guinea yielded rich treasure, and beyond were the Indies and the Spanish main. At home, manufactures were stimulated by the plentifulness of money, and the consequent rise in prices. Busy towns rose in the north. Manchester began to be celebrated for its friezes, York for its coverlets, Sheffield for its cutlery. Agriculture also benefited. Arable farming was increasing, partly because the higher prices once more rendered it profitable, partly because, from over-production, the price of wool had fallen. The new landlords who held the old Church lands employed more capital in the work, and by manuring and such scientific methods so improved their holdings, that one acre yielded as much as two had done before. This more expensive farming employed more hands, so the banished labourers were gradually returning to the land.

From this general view of Elizabeth's reign we must now turn to the phase of activity in which we are especially interested, namely, what one might almost call the epidemic of building, which spread over the land. Everywhere new buildings were being erected. People's ideas of comfort had been revolutionised; they were rolling in wealth, comparatively speaking; the gentlemen were all building new manors; the farmers, new farmhouses; the labourers, new cottages.

Nearly all the old half-timbered cottages we see to-day were built within the hundred years from 1550 to 1650, and the busiest time of all seems to have been between the years 1575 and 1625. After 1650 the impulse seemed to die away, and there was little new building of cottages. The old buildings were merely added to and altered as time went on, until we come right down to the nineteenth century, when the bare, cheerless barracks which seem to typify the factory system came into existence. But the cottages belong to the homelier days of hand labour, when the commercial spirit was new, and had not turned everything to dross in its search for gold.

We are fortunate in possessing a graphic account of this great expansion of building, not compiled from old records, but written by a contemporary. For in the first volume of Holinshed's *Chronicle*, published in 1577, we have a capital description of the state of England under Queen Elizabeth, written by William Harrison, rector of a little village in Essex. Honest man, though writing of England at

large, he prefers, when possible, to speak of the things
he has actually seen, and to draw his illustrations
from his own village. He is a curious mixture of
simplicity and shrewdness, and speaks with some
misgivings of the changes which have taken place
in his day. His matter is so interesting, and so
quaintly and pithily expressed, that I shall make
no apology for quoting him largely in the following
pages.

' Never so much oke,' he says, ' hath been spent
in a hundred years before as in ten years of our time,
for everie man almost is a builder, and he that hath
bought any small parcel of ground, be it ever so
little, will not be quiet till he have pulled downe the
old house, if anie were there standing, and set up a
new after his own device.'

Apart from the general prosperity there were many
reasons for this building. For the previous hundred
years, cottages had been systematically pulled
down, as more and more land went out of cultivation
and was placed under pasture. The population was
now almost double what it had been sixty years
before, and, as we have seen, the labourers were coming back to the land. Housing accommodation was
urgently needed, and the building of cottages was

largely a necessity. Over and above this, men seemed to build for the love of it.

'It is a world to see,' says Harrison, 'how diverse men being bent to building and having a delectable vein in spending of their goods by that trade, doo dailie imagine new devices of their owne to guide their workmen withall, and these more curious and excellent alwaies than the former. In the proceeding also of their workes how they set up, how they pull downe, how they enlarge, how they restreine, how they ad to, how they take from, whereby their heads are never idle, their purses never shut, nor their bookes of account never made perfect.'

And the new houses were much better than the old. In a most interesting passage he reviews at length the changes taking place, all in the direction of greater comfort or increased luxury.

'The ancient manors and houses of our gentlemen are yet and for the most part of strong timber, in framing whereof our carpenters have been and are worthilie preferred before those of like science among all other nations. Howbeit such as be latelie builded are commonlie either of bricke or hard stone or both; their roomes large and comelie, and houses of office further distant from their lodgings. Those

of the nobilitie are likewise wrought with brick and
hard stone as provision may best be made ; but so
magnificent and statelie as the basest house of a
baron doth often match in our daies with some
honours of princes in old time. So that if ever
curious building did florish in England it is in these
our years, wherein our workmen excell. . . . Never-
theless their estimation more than their greedie and
servile covetousnesse, joined with a lingering
humour ' (how this hits off the British working-man),
' causeth them often to be rejected, and strangers
preferred to greater bargains, who are more reasonable in their takings, and lesse wasters of time by a
greate deale than our own. The furniture of our
houses also exceedeth and is grown in manner even
to passing delicacie, and herein I doo not speake of the
nobilitie and gentrie onlie, but likewise of the lowest
sort in most places of our south countrie, that have
anie thing at all to take to. Certes in noblemen's
houses it is not rare to see abundance of arras, rich
hangings of tapestrie, silver vessell, and so much
other plate as may furnish sundrie cupbords, to the
summe often times of a thousand or two thousand
pounds at the least : whereby the value of this and
the rest of their stuff dooth grow to be almost in-

estimable. Likewise in the houses of knights, gentlemen, merchant men, and some other wealthie
citizens, it is not geson to behold generallie their
great provision of tapistrie, Turkie work, pewter,
brasse, fine linen, and thereto costlie cupbords of
plate worth five or six hundred or a thousand
pounds to be deemed by estimation. But as herein
all these sorts doo far exceed their elders and pre-
decessors, and in neatness and curiositie the merchant
all other, so in time past the costlie furniture staied
there, whereas now it is descended yet lower, even
unto the inferior artificers and manie farmers who, by
virtue of their old and not of their new leases, have
for the most part learned also to garnish their
cupbords with plate, their beds with tapistrie and
silke hangings, and their tables with carpets and
fine naperie, whereby the wealth of our countrie,
God be praised therefore, and give us grace to
emploie it well, dooth infinitelie appeare.'

Not that this prosperity touched every one. The
agricultural labourers working for hire suffered
greatly by the rise in prices, for their wages were
forbidden to rise by Act of Parliament. Persons
with fixed incomes were in a similar position, and
this was the case with poor Harrison himself, whose

slender stipend of forty pounds was worth less and less each year. No wonder that he found it rather hard to rejoice in a state of well-being in which he had so little share, and that a rather pathetic note finds its way into the next paragraph.

' Neither do I speake this in reproch of anie man. God is my judge but to shew that I do rejoice rather, to see how God hath blessed us with his good gifts : and whilest I behold how that in a time wherein all things are growen to most excessive prices, we doo yet find the means to obtain and atchive such furniture as heretofore hath beene unpossible. There are old men yet dwelling in the village where I remaine, which have noted three things to be marvellouslie altered in England, within their sound remembrance ; one is the multitude of chimnies latelie erected, whereas in their young daies there was not above two or three, if so manie, in most uplandish townes of the realme, the religious houses, and manour places of their lords alwaies excepted, and peradventure some great personages, but ech one made his fire against a reredosse in the hall, where he dined and dressed his meate.

' The second is the great though not general amendment of lodging, for, said they, our fathers and we ourselves also have lien full oft upon straw pallets, on rough mats, covered onelie with a sheet, under coverlets made of dogswain, or hapharlots (I use their own termes), and a good round log under their heads in steed of a bolster or pillow. If it were so that our fathers or the good man of the house had within seven years after his marriage purchased a mattress or flocke-bed, and thereto a sacke of chaffe to rest his head upon, he thought himselfe to be as well lodged as the lord of the towne, that peradventure laie seldome in a bed of downe or whole fethers ; so well were they contented and with such base kind of furniture, which also is not verie much amended as yet in some parts of Bedfordshire, and elsewhere further off from our southern parts. Pillows, said they, were thought meet onelie for women in child-bed. As for servants, if they had anie sheet above them, it was well, for seldome had they anie under their bodies to keepe them from the pricking straws that ran oft through the canvas of the pallet, and rased their hardened hides.

'The third thing they tell of is the exchange of vessell as of treene platters into pewter, and wooden spoones into silver or tin. For so common were all sorts of treene stuffe in old time, that a man should hardlie find foure pieces of pewter of which one was peradventure a salt, in a good farmer's house, and yet for all this frugalitie, if it may so be justly called, they were scarce able to live and pay their rentes at their daies without selling of a cow, or an horse, or more, although they paid but foure pounds at the uttermost by the yeare. Such also was their povertie, that if some one od farmer or husbandmen had been at the ale-house, a thing greatlie used in those daies, amongst six or seven of his neighbours, and there in a braverie to shew what store he had, did cast downe his purse, and therein a noble or six shillings in silver unto them, for few such men cared for gold, because it was not so readie payment, and they were oft enforced to give a penie for the exchange of an angell, it was verie likelie that all the rest could not laie downe so much against it : whereas in my time, although peradventure foure pounds of old rent be improved to fortie, fiftie, or an hundred pounds, yet will the farmer as another palme or date tree, thinke his gaines verie small toward the middest of his terme if he have not six or seven yeares' rent lieing by him, therewith to purchase a new lease, beside a faire garnish of pewter on his cupbord, with so much more in od vessell going about the house, three or foure

feather beds, so manie coverlids, and carpets of
tapistrie, a silver salt, a bowle for wine, if not an
whole neast, and a dozzen of spoones to furnish up
the sute. This also he taketh to be his own cleere,
for what stocke of monie soever he gathereth and
laieth up in all his yeares, it is often seen, that the
landlord will take such order with him for the same,
when he reneweth his lease (which is commonlie
eight or ten yeares before the old be expyred, but it
is now growen almost to a custome that if he come
not to his lord so long before another shall step in for
a reversion), and so defeat him out right, that it shall
never trouble him more than the haire of his beard,
when the barber hath washed and shaved it from
his chin.'

Certainly we get from this an insight into the
methods of the landlord, but, after all, from Harrison's
own account, the farmer seems to have prospered in
spite of them.

But in the opinion of the honest rector these changes
were not entirely for the public good. Effeminate
luxury he considers many of them, and he goes on
to talk of the good old days when wants were fewer,
life simpler, and men more hardy.

' Albeit that there were then greater number of

messuages and mansions almost in every place, yet were their frames so slight and slender that one meane dwelling-house in our time is able to counter-vaile verie manie of them, if you consider the present change with the plentie of timber that we bestow upon them. In times past men were contented to dwell in houses builded of sallow, willow, plum-tree, hardbeane, and elme, so that the use of oke was in maner dedicated wholie unto churches, religious houses, princes' palaces, noblemen's lodgings, and navigation, but now all these are rejected, and nothing but oke anie whit regarded. And yet see the change, for when our houses were builded of willow, then had we oken men, but now that our houses are come to be made of oke, our men are not onelie become willow, but a great manie, through Persian delicacy crept in among us, altogether straw, which is a sore alteration. In those days the courage of the owner was a sufficient defence to keepe the house in safetie ' [one might hint that it was also in all probability not worth robbing], ' but now the assurance of the timber double doores, lockes, and bolts, must defend the man from robbing. Now have we manie chimnies, and yet our tenderlings complaine of rheumes, catarhs, and poses. Then had we none

but reredoses, and our heads did never ake. For as
the smoke in these daies was supposed to be a
sufficient harding for the timber of the house, so it
was reputed a far better medicine to keepe the
goodman and his familie from the quacke or pose,
wherewith as then verie few were oft acquainted.'

Just as the old rector marks the 'lingering
humour' of the workman, so he is down on him for
scamping his work.

'This furthermore,' he remarks, 'among other
things I have to saie of our husbandmen and artificers,
that they were never so excellent in their trades as
at this present. But as the workmanship of the
later sort was never more fine and curious to the
eie, so was it never lesse strong and substantial for
continuance and benefit to the buiers. Certes there
is nothing that hurteth the common sort of our
artificers more than hast and a barbarous or slavish
desire to turn the penie, and by ridding their worke
to make speedie utterance of their wares, which
enforceth them to bungle of, and dispatch manie
things they care not how, so they be out of their
hands, whereby the buier is often sore defrauded and
findeth to his cost that " hast maketh wast "
according to the proverbe.'

Even where it did not result in the scamping of work, the increased demand for houses had a distinct effect on the style of building erected. In the older work, barge-boards, door-posts and other prominent timbers were often richly carved, but now there was no time for such refinements. Where ornament was required, we find mouldings used instead of carving. There soon began also to be a shortness in the supply of timber. Harrison foresaw this, and says that there are four things that he would fain see reformed in his lifetime. Two of these refer to the backslidings of his flock, to the want of discipline in church, and the holding of markets and fairs on Sundays, but the other two are more personal and characteristic. One is a protectionist proposal that merchants should be made to sell home produce rather than foreign, but the last is the wisest of all. It is that every one owning forty acres of land or more should plant one acre of wood. It reminds one of the maxim of the old laird of Dumbiedykes. ' Aye be pitten in a tree,' he says to his son ; ' it will be growin' while you 're sleepin'.' But it is a vain wish, as he knows. ' I feare me,' he says quaintly, ' that I should then live too long, and so long that I should either be wearie of the world or the world of me, and yet they are not such thyngs but they may easilie be brought to passe.' So with these words of homely wisdom on his lips we take leave of the kindly old man.

His forebodings were soon realised. To such an extent did the scarcity of timber grow that in 1604 a proclamation was issued in London, forbidding its use in the fronts of houses, which with the windows were to be entirely of brick and stone; and similar laws were made in 1624 and again in 1630.

But the evil cured itself. With the first half of the seventeenth century the cottage building came to an end. Since then we have had stately and elegant homes of the Queen Anne and Georgian styles, but no more old cottages. The time for them had passed away.

We have now traced rapidly the evolution of the English cottage. From its earliest beginnings in the rude hut of the early Britons we have followed its gradual growth. We have seen how each change in the social condition of the people was reflected in their homes. How the cottage was all but swallowed up by the great hall in the feudal days, to reappear in an improved form when feudalism died away, and a class of independent yeomen arose.

And finally we have seen it reach maturity in the moments when England first touched greatness, and assumed her place in the van of the world's progress.

After that there was nothing left for it but to grow old. But as the daffodils ' take the winds of March with beauty,' so do the cottages bow under the hand of age. Like good wine they have mellowed with years. Fresh and bright as they must have been in all their morning's glory, yet they are more interesting now in the evening of their days. They seem saturated with human experience. And just as a coat that has been worn for long seems to take on the mould of the wearer, so they seem to express the lives that have been lived within their walls.

CHAPTER V

THE STRUCTURE

'Not a log in this building but its memories has got,
And not a nail in this old floor but touches a tender spot.'
                                    WILL CARLETON.

IT is time now to examine a little more in detail the structure of the old cottage. And though the surviving examples, with few exceptions, date from the same period, the hundred years from 1550 to 1650, yet they present considerable variety of form and size, some being almost as simple as the primitive hut of the thirteenth century, others but little less comfortable and commodious than the manor-house of Elizabethan days. For, as frequently happens in such cases, the older styles, when improved upon, did not die out. They continued to be built, and merely fell one grade lower in the social scale. The yeoman's house of the one generation may serve as the model of the cottar's dwelling in the next, just as we often see the old manor-house actually degraded to the position of a farmhouse as time goes on.

If one refers to Chaucer's description of the poor widow's dwelling in the Nun's Priest's Tale, one finds it differs little from that of Bishop Hall of the copyholder's house, written about two hundred years later.

'A poore wydwé,' it begins, 'somdel stape in age, was whilom dwellying in a narwe cottage.' She was a woman of some modest property, for 'Three large sowes hadde she, and namo, three keen and eek a sheepe,' but her lodging was of the most primitive kind, a mere 'but and a ben.' 'Full sooty was her bower, and eek hir halle.'

Now turn to Bishop Hall on the home of the miserable copyholder of Elizabethan days :

'Of one bay's breadth God wot a silly cote
Whose thatched spars are furred with sluttish soote,
A whole inch thick, shining like blackmore's brows
Through smoke that downe the headlesse barrell blows.
At his bed's head feaden his stalled teame,
His swine beneath his pullen o'er the beame.'

This sounds just as poor and much more squalid than the poor widow's cottage, which at least had separate accommodation for the poultry. 'A yeerd she hadde, encloséd al aboute, with stikkes and a dryé ditch without.'

The normal plan of the oldest and most primitive cottages remaining is a simple parallelogram. Such a cottage contained only two rooms, one on the ground-floor and a sleeping-apartment under the roof, sometimes reached not by a stair but by a ladder.

The plan of the yeoman's cottage of the sixteenth and early seventeenth centuries is somewhat more elaborate. It is based on the mediæval manor-house. In the centre is an oblong common room or hall, the successor of the old lofty hall which used to run right up to the roof. On each side of this are rooms forming wings, which project a little. The upper story in the early examples overhangs the lower, and often the roof is carried from wing to wing, over the central recess. A very fine example of an early sixteenth-century house of this style may be seen at Pattenden in Kent, which was built for the standard-bearer of Henry VIII.

A smaller type of cottage has often only two rooms on the ground-floor, parlour and kitchen, the door entering a small hall or porch between the two ; while above are the sleeping-apartments. In most cases, however, the original plan has been rather obscured by subsequent additions. The roof is often continued almost to the ground behind, or at the sides, the additional space thus obtained—called a lean-to—being utilised for sculleries, pantries, or other similar purposes.

In some later cottages we find the plan is much more irregular, and the structures become more rambling, and in some cases it is modified by the peculiarities of the site, but the most common type of all periods is based on the simple parallelogram, with or without wings.

At the time of the great cottage building, England was still essentially a wooded country, and wood was the general building material, the local carpenter being architect and builder combined. Brick alone had not come into general use, though in Elizabethan times and later largely used in conjunction with a timber framework. Stone was little used even where quarries were at hand, for, as a rule, it was easier and cheaper to use wood.

So the typical old cottage is what we call a ' half-timbered ' or ' post and panel ' building, made up of a framework of timbers, filled in with either brick-work, wattle and daub, or a plaster of any material ready to hand.

The foundation is of stone, though often carried very little above the surface of the ground, so that the bottom horizontal beam almost rests on the ground, as may be seen on reference to the plate facing page 154.[1] Any stone that was easily obtainable was used, and in later cottages the foundation is often of brick.

The making of the frame was the most important part of the building of such a house. The wood used was almost invariably oak. The main posts were massive timbers of from eight to ten inches square, the intermediate posts not square in section, but varying from about six by two and a half inches to eight by four inches. Those carrying the second floor and the roof were also great square beams.

The frames seem to have been fitted together by the carpenter and kept in his yard, probably to season, for some time before being set up. At least so one would judge from an Act of the time of Henry VIII. directed against 'the secret burning of frames of timber prepared and made by the owners thereof ready to be set up and edified for houses.'

The setting up of the frame was an occasion of rejoicing, just as the laying of the foundation-stone is in the case of a stone building. In Addy's *Evolution of the English House*, an account for the building of a house in Sheffield in 1575 is given, and in it occurs an item of £2, 6s. 8d. 'for meate and drinke that day the house was reared,' *i.e.* the frame

1. Plate 35 in this edition

set up—a considerable sum if we remember the difference in the value of money in those days.

In fixing the frames together nails were not used, the beams being firmly knitted together by mortice and tendon. As has already been pointed out, in early work the posts are close together, getting wider apart as time goes on and timber becomes scarcer. Even at an early date Harrison notes that the panels are closer in well-wooded districts than in those where timber is less plentiful.

There is something very beautiful about some of these massive frames. Formerly, of course, as traced in Chapter II., the framework consisted merely of two ' gavel ' forks joined together by a ridge-pole and horizontal beams, like the skeleton of a ship. In primitive cottages the same form may still be seen to-day, as in the plate facing page 84,[1] and there is great beauty in its simple lines. But as the structure becomes more complex, the positions of the great beams are more and more cunningly devised. Designed on scientific principles, however unconscious the science may be, such a framework has both beauty and strength. In it we see the very bones of the house. And though in the first place these timbers are essentially structural, each contributing its part to the stability

1. Plate 18 in this edition

of the fabric, yet one of the most pleasing features of cottage architecture is the way they are turned to decorative use. In the later examples, particularly in Lancashire, Cheshire, and Shropshire, this decoration often becomes very ornate. The panels are filled with designs, often a circle round the intersection of the posts, and for this work the crooked boughs and roots of trees are deftly utilised.

Nothing, indeed, could be more ingenious than the way those gnarled and twisted pieces of timber are worked in by the builders. In the older cottages they used the root part in the massive door-posts which branched out overhead and supported the projecting upper story. As Harrison says : ' Such is their husbandrie in dealing with their timber that the same stuffe which in time past was rejected as crooked, unprofitable, and to no use but the fire, dooth now come in the front and best part of the work, whereby the common saieing is likewise in these daies verified in our mansion-houses, which earst was said only of the timber for ships, that ' no oke can grow so crooked but it falleth out to some use.'

In the north country these beams have, as a rule, been tarred to preserve them from the effects of the weather, and their staring black-and-white appearance has led to the houses being termed 'magpies,' but this tarring is all of recent date. The wood was originally left untouched, and few tints are more exquisite than the silver-grey of the old weathered oak. This silvery quality is well brought out in Mrs. Allingham's drawings, particularly in the plates facing pages 142 and 146.[1]

The oldest way of filling in the panels was with 'wattle and daub.' This was done as follows. Upright hazel rods were fixed in grooves cut in the horizontal timbers, and then thinner hazel wands were twisted hurdlewise round them. The panel was then filled in with a plaster of marly clay and chopped straw, and finished with a coat of lime plaster. In most cases the outside was finished flush with the face of the posts, though in some old examples it was set back half an inch, and the corner of the projecting post moulded. Within, the plaster-work only extended to the thickness of the thinner intermediate posts, leaving the main post projecting. In inside partitions, however, the plaster was usually the whole thickness of the main posts.

Brick in the later work is often used as a filling for the panels, especially in Surrey and Kent. Sometimes the bricks are laid fancifully in herring-bone pattern,

1. Plates 32 and 33 in this edition

but this is not a style suitable for exposure to the weather. Sometimes the brick-work is plastered over, probably at a subsequent date, and when the plaster begins to fall off in patches, as it usually does, and reveals the red brick underneath, the effect is very pleasing, as, for example, in the plate facing page 16[1]

It is rather a strange thing that within the last fifty years we should have returned to a system of building which is practically the old method of putting together a strong frame, and then merely filling in the panels. But there is this difference, that where the old builder used oak, we use steel. It is rather difficult to say why in modern hands this style of construction yields results that are so unbeautiful. In most cases the problem is shirked by concealing the framework, the fabric being apparently supported by the walls, which to all appearance are of sufficient strength to bear the strain, and so the eye is satisfied. Though where in a street the first-floor is merely supported on steel struts and the whole front filled in with plate-glass, the effect is very disturbing ; the whole building looks as if it were standing on the edges of the sheets of glass. The root of the trouble lies in the fact that the steel girder is not an ordinary product of nature, and so the eye gives

1. Plate 5 in this edition

us no clue to its strength. During the passing of many generations we have acquired a sort of sub-conscious knowledge of the weight a beam of wood will bear. In the living tree we have seen the proportion of the trunk to the mass of foliage above, and have watched the huge bulk sway in the wind, and we have known it to fall with a crash when the strain became too great. With stonework the impression given to the eye is of a substance solid as rock, and so long as the proportions give no feeling of top-heaviness or lack of balance, the eye is satisfied there. But the steel girder is so slim that there appears something unnatural in its strength, something that puts it out of tune with surrounding nature. It is this last that is the real reason for its ugliness. It is out of harmony with nature; the more artificial its environment, the better it looks; the more it comes into contact with untamed nature, the worse it appears. Nothing seems more utterly incongruous than the great steel bridges that cross the mountain torrents on the Pacific Railway, amid the stupendous natural forms that surround them, yet the same bridge in the midst of a manufacturing town would be comparatively inoffensive.

And so while the wooden frames of the old builder

were boldly placed in full view, and partly from their fine design, partly from the beauty of their natural lines, partly from their exquisite colour, became a source of pleasure to the onlooker, we hide our steel frames away. Their slightness looks absurd, like a mere spider's web ; the lines of the metal are all too rigid, its surface wants the interest and texture which gives charm to the oaken beam. Perhaps, after all, to conceal them is the wisest thing we can do.

The old walls, though so picturesque, were not always water-tight, and we find them protected in various ways. The modern system, as effective as it is ugly, is to case the whole building in a sheath of cement, a treatment which kills almost every element of external beauty with the exception of fine proportion, which always remains. In this guise one has no clue from the outside as to what the interior may be, and sometimes a most unprepossessing husk will hide a delightful kernel. Just as among the volumes of a public library, where everything is bound alike in the same serviceable but inartistic covers, at one moment we may handle a work of modern fiction, at another a rare old classic, but both are alike till we peep inside.

In the past their devices, though possibly less effective, were, at any rate, much more decorative. In Surrey and Kent especially a custom prevailed of covering the walls with tiles, wherever additional protection from the weather was desired. These weather-tiles, as they were called, were hung on oak laths nailed to battens, and were bedded in mortar. This is much more durable than simply nailing the tiles to the boarding, which in that case is rather apt to decay. The tilers sometimes followed the latter system as it was so much easier then to get the rows of tiles straight. The slight irregularity, however, caused by the bedding in mortar, rather adds to the appearance by taking away the machine-like rigidity of the line.

Weather-tiling is not of very ancient date. Professor Rogers mentions ' wall-tiles ' as occurring in the sixteenth-century accounts. Perhaps these were weather-tiles, but much more probably the term merely applied to ordinary bricks. Most weather-tiles date from no earlier a period than the beginning of the eighteenth century, for it was not till the cottages were old and falling into disrepair that they were required.

Still, though it formed no part of the building as

originally designed, there is no doubt that the cottages of Surrey and Kent owe to their weather-tiling much of their beauty. There is something particularly rich and glowing in the colour which the old tile assumes, and the wall-tiles seem to develop and retain this colour more than the roof-tiles which are exposed to the direct rays of the sun and the continual washing of rain.

Sometimes the tiles are quite plain, at other times their lower edges are cut into fanciful shapes. The little town of Haslemere especially is famous for its variety of ornamental weather-tiles, several forms being found there which are not known elsewhere. But these ornate forms are best used in conjunction with rows of plain tiles, which have a steadying effect, and prevent the surface being broken up in too distracting a manner.

In the plate facing page 278[1] we have an example of the Haslemere weather-tiling at its best. Rows of plain and ornamental tiles alternate, and the six bottom rows, which are plain, project in a characteristic fashion to form a sort of hood, and throw off the rain from the lower part of the wall. In the plate facing this page[2] we have a less elaborate but still more extensive piece of weather-tiling from Edenbridge in Kent.

1. Plate 63 in this edition
2. Plate 20

Another covering of a similar sort, less ornamental
and probably less permanent, is weather-boarding.
But there is something very pleasant in a large
expanse of these flat boards, turned by exposure to
a pale-grey colour, or where they have been tarred
as a protection against the weather, taking on deep
shades of purple and blue. The planks, often of
elm, are as a rule just sawn out of the log without
their edges being dressed, and the natural wavy lines
break the monotony of the surface with a charming
irregularity.

Weather-boarding was frequently applied to the
outbuildings that cluster round a farmyard, and
which in their sobriety form an excellent foil to the
brighter and more gaily coloured farmhouse. Unfortunately these old outhouses are fast disappearing,
and are being replaced by hideous structures of
corrugated iron.

Having considered at some length the walls of the
cottage, let us now turn our attention to the roof,
which, from a decorative point of view, is the chief
feature of the building. Indeed, a well-known
architect, Mr. Ralph Nevill, F.S.A., in his interesting
volume on cottage architecture, says that the chief
lesson to be gained from the study of the old work

is to be found in their careful grouping of roof forms.

The chief characteristic of the roofs of the older and smaller cottages is their extreme simplicity. They are high-pitched, and unbroken by either dormer windows or gables, the normal form being what is called a hipped roof. That is, the roof runs downward and outward from the ridge-pole, not only to the front and back, but to the sides as well ; but a glance at the plates facing pages 98 and 107 will render further explanation unnecessary.[1]

The pitch of the roof is generally a good guide to the age of a cottage, the earlier ones being very steep, those of the late sixteenth and the seventeenth centuries much flatter. Roofs with many gables are characteristic of Elizabeth's reign, when the simplicity of the old form gives place to the interest of more elaborate designs.

The hipped roof, however, is the common form in all early work. Sometimes the hip is continued right down to within a few feet of the ground, on one or both sides, as may be seen in the old farmhouse in the plate facing page 190, or the Kentish cottage in the plate facing page 138.[2]

But simple as these old roofs look, there are many

1. Plates 21 and 24 in this edition
2. Plates 45 and 31

PLATE 17. THE HIGH COTTAGE

PLATE 20. THE DAIRY FARM, EDENBRIDGE, KENT

PLATE 21. AT QUIDHAMPTON, NEAR SALISBURY

PLATE 22. COTTAGE NEAR FARRINGFORD, I.W.

PLATE 23. BACKS, GODALMING

PLATE 24. OLD SUSSEX COTTAGE

little touches about them that add just that spice of piquancy that makes the difference between the interesting and the commonplace. The junction of the top of the hip with the main roof is one of these. The hip rafters cannot, of course, all run up to the ridge-pole; there is not room, so they start from a point about nine inches below the ridge. Between the ridge-pole and the top of the hip, there is left a little gablet which gives spirit to the roof. This, of course, refers to tiled roofs only ; in the case of thatch, main roof and hip are merged in one unbroken fold.

Where gables are introduced, and these occur as early as the fifteenth century, though still more common in the sixteenth and seventeenth, we have a new feature, the barge-boards, two stout beams underlying the covering of thatch or tiles, and carrying it out from the wall a few inches to allow the drip to fall clear. With a fine instinct these beams were often richly ornamented, especially in the examples of the fifteenth and early sixteenth centuries, when we find them elaborately carved, or pierced in quaint patterns of trefoils, cusps, and other devices. A fine specimen may be seen at Penshurst, in the house adjoining the churchyard, but such old Gothic work is comparatively rare. With the great rush of building in Elizabeth's reign, the carpenter had not time to execute these elaborately carved barge-boards, and from that date onwards we find, instead of the Gothic carvings, laboriously wrought by hand, Renaissance mouldings, which could be quickly executed in the piece, and afterwards cut up as required. Thus even at this early date we see the conflict between art and commercialism.

In the plate facing page 154[1] is a very good example of the Gothic barge-board, marking the cottage it adorns as not later in date than the first part of the sixteenth century. Additional evidence of the age of the building may be seen in the closeness of the posts and in the overhanging top story.

The thatched roof is probably the earliest roof form of all. I should think it originated in the covering with turf of the early rude wicker huts ; the growing grass on the turf would turn off the rain, and indeed, as it dried, it would assume much the appearance of ordinary thatch.

Now from north to south, from the Highlands of Scotland to the wealds of Surrey and Kent, wherever we find a primitive dwelling we find a thatched roof. It may be the material varies, heather in one part, straw in another, rushes in a third, but it is still thatch.

1. Plate 35 in this edition

It is applied to all styles of building. You will find it on the half-timbered cottages of the woodlands, the stone cottages of the Cotswolds, or the mud-walled cottages of Wessex. In some districts, tile or the Horsham stone slates may supplant it, but still it is the most general roof-covering for the old cottages.

There is something indescribably cosy about a thatched roof. It seems to wrap a house round like a blanket, and speaks convincingly of warmth and comfort. It softens out all the angularities from the roof-lines, smooths them over with the gentle curves of a snow-drift ; the dormer windows become little peep-holes like birds' nests, and the overhanging eaves are full of sparrows. And this appearance of snugness is no deception. To one accustomed to the old thatch, a slate or even tile roof is a change for the worse, colder in winter and hotter in summer, for the thatch, like a thick, shaggy hide, is a good non-conductor, and keeps out equally heat and cold.

The great drawback to the use of thatch is the danger of fire, and this has led to its almost entire disuse in towns. In mediæval times the thatch used to be whitewashed as a protection against this danger, and a strange appearance such a roof must have had amid the green foliage. One almost wishes the custom might be revived! It would give an English village something the appearance of a Moorish settlement, though the arid surroundings would be lacking, and the blazing African sun.

In country districts, however, where houses stand isolated, the danger is less, and despite the reports that the thatcher's is a fast-disappearing industry, in almost every part of England one will see patches of new thatch, and even whole roofs of fresh yellow straw, testifying to his activity.

In a little Wiltshire village I found an old thatcher. It was a little hamlet away to the south of Salisbury, where the sleepy country life seemed to run on much the same lines as a hundred years ago. A pleasant rolling country full of pasture-land, with the distant spire of the cathedral town amidst its green woodlands shimmering in the heat haze.

The thatcher was a man of sixty, hale and hearty. His father, a thatcher, had just died at the age of eighty, and his grandfather had been a thatcher too. So far from the old industry dying out, he told me he had more work than he could do, for there was no competition, and he was bringing up his nephew to follow the same trade.

At first he was too diffident to talk much, but when ensconced in a tiny ale-house—he would not go to the larger and more fashionable establishment, but took me to this quiet corner where he could guarantee the excellence of the tap—he soon began to tell me all I wanted to know about his work. Not content with that, he went out to the courtyard behind, where there was a thatched lean-to, and gave a practical demonstration, and finished up by taking me to his little cottage to inspect the home-made tools which he used.

The system is as follows. The thatch is laid direct on the rafters. Stout rods as thick as a man's thumb and about four feet long, called ledgers, are interlaced in the rafters, and on these the thatch is laid in bundles, and tied down with stout tarred cord. The thatcher works from the eaves up to the ridge, and at the ridge the straw is bent over and carried down the other side. The straw is preferably wheat straw, and the best length is about four feet. Rye straw is sometimes used, but it is not so good. Good straw of any kind is difficult to procure now, as in these days of machine-reaping it gets bruised and broken. The life of the machine-reaped straw is about a third of that reaped by hand in the old-fashioned way.

Heather is often used for thatch and has a very neat and trim appearance, though rather sooty in colour.

The first coat of thatch should last some six or seven years. It is then time to add another coat. This is simply laid on the top of the first, and secured by what is called sparring. A stout rod is laid horizontally on the top of the new layer ; then hazel pins, about two feet long, well toughened by soaking in water, and sharpened at both ends, are bent double in the form of huge hairpins, and driven in with a mallet, one prong on each side of the hazel rod, so as to bind it firmly down. These pins are driven in about a foot apart, and thus the two layers of thatch held closely together.

There are generally two rows of this sparring at the top on each side of the roof-ridge, and one at the foot, just above the eaves, as may be seen clearly in the plate facing this page[1]. Often, however, extra rows of sparring are added round dormer windows, or wherever extra binding is required, and ornamental patterns are worked out, such as herring-boning, as in the example already referred to.

1. Plate 22 in this edition

This second layer should last from twelve to fourteen years, and when a third is required, should be stripped off, so that the new layer may be pinned direct to the first. But the old system often was to lay three or four layers, one on top of the other, and this is still done ; and certainly the thicker the thatch the finer the effect.

When the straw is laid on, it is combed or raked down to make it smooth. The old thatcher's rake was a most primitive instrument, consisting merely of a stout ash rod with a number of large nails driven through it to form the teeth. After being combed down, the thatch is trimmed with a flat knife mounted on a handle like that of a builder's trowel. The eaves are then cut square with a hook like a reaping-hook, and finished off with shears.

Damp weather is best for thatching, as then the straw works in more closely together. Frosty weather and great heat are bad, for in both these cases the straw becomes brittle.

So much I learned from my talk with old Mr. Musselwhite. I was surprised to see, when he pulled to pieces a bit of old thatch, that grey as was the surface layer, the inside straw was still bright and golden as the day it was reaped. One could find quite a pretty little moral in the fact that those quiet grey roofs are all rich gold underneath.

In some districts, particularly in Surrey and Kent, the tiled roof is more common than thatch. Tiles were first imported from the Netherlands, but they were made in England at an early date, being manufactured in Essex and Suffolk in the fourteenth century.

They were employed first in the towns, owing to the greater security they afforded against fire, and by the middle of the fifteenth century they had become quite common. In some towns their use was enforced by law, and there was such a demand for them that often they were difficult to obtain, and we hear of a case in 1472, when buildings had to be left for a time unroofed as tiles could not be had at any price. ' There were none to get for no money.'

The corporation of Reading in 1443 passed a quaint bye-law, calculated to guard against the danger of fire in two ways. It seems that the barbers of the town were in the habit of shaving customers at late hours by candle-light, and it was decreed ' that no barber shall keep his shop open or shave any man after ten o'clock between Easter and Michaelmas, nor after nine from Michaelmas to Easter, except he be a stranger or town worthy ' (one would like to know the definition of 'town worthy'), 'on pain of being fined three hundred tiles to the Guildhall, to be received by the cofferers.' Instances of payment are entered in the town records.

When tiles are laid, the laths to which they are attached are made of heart of oak. So durable is this wood that, except where the corrosion of iron nails has rotted them, the laths are in most cases quite sound. The old tilers did not use nails on that account, but pins of hazel and willow, or what was specially prized, pins made out of an old elder stump. The making of these pins was a useful occupation for the tiler in winter when the severity of the weather stopped his ordinary work.

Much of the beauty of the old tiled roofs is due to their irregularity. Partly this is the result merely of decay, the main parts having rotted at the foundation, and the fabric settled down in a picturesque, but rather uncomfortable fashion; also the spars on which the tiles are fastened sag down between the rafters, so that the ridge line rises and falls in curves, and the roof is full of hills and hollows. Partly also it is due to the fact that the tiles were not turned out with the precision of the modern machine-made article. They varied slightly in size and in thickness, and so an old tiled roof has all the charm of broken colour, as compared with the monotonous, flat tint of the new, and its lines are not straight as drawn with a ruler, but wave pleasantly. Nowadays, however, it is possible to obtain hand-made tiles which have something of the quality of the old, and respond to the influence of the weather in a more kindly manner than the ordinary produce of the modern brick-field.

A third roof-covering which is largely used in Surrey and in Sussex is formed of slabs of slaty stone, known as Horsham slabs. Thicker and larger than slates, and of a cool grey colour, these slabs have a quiet beauty of their own, more restful than the rich red tiles, more dignified in their ruggedness than the soft and rather shapeless thatch.

The pitch of the roof when they are used is flatter, owing to their great weight, and on this account such roofs are apt to be less water-tight than those thatched or tiled. The slabs vary in size, the largest being next the eaves, and they decrease as one goes up to the ridge. The ridge itself is often capped with ridge tiles. An excellent idea of the appearance of a roof of Horsham slabs may be obtained from the plate facing page 154.[1]

1. Plate 35 in this edition

In the preceding plate is another example, curious in this respect, that the main roof is covered with Horsham slabs, while the hip at the side, evidently added at a subsequent period, is roofed with tile.

Such roofs are becoming less and less numerous. When they fall into disrepair they are seldom restored to their old condition, but have the slabs replaced by the lighter and more convenient tiles.

Another roof-covering formerly largely used was oak shingles, but, except in a few church-spires, I have not seen any actual examples, though I understand such still exist. Those shingle roofs must have been much less durable than tile or stone slabs, though their lightness will explain their being used on such very steep roofs as one necessarily finds on the steeple of a church.

In Devonshire small, grey stone tiles (or slabs) are common, while slates are used in the Cotswolds and many other places.

CHAPTER VI

THE STRUCTURE (*continued*)

'Fare you well, old house, you're nought that can feel or see,
But you seem like a human being—a dear old friend to me.'
                                                WILL CARLETON.

As the roof itself is the most important part of the cottage from a decorative standpoint, so is the chimney the culminating feature of the roof. Its spiral of smoke first catches our eye in the distance, and when we approach nearer, its tall, well-proportioned shaft gives a distinction to the simple roof.

It is very instructive to find how things which seem to us the merest commonplaces, and which appear as if they must always have existed, are really the result of long centuries of slow growth. Though to us a chimney seems a necessary adjunct to a house, it does not appear in English domestic architecture until quite a late period. The evolution of the chimney gives us in a nutshell the growth of domestic comfort in England.

The primitive system, as we have seen, was to build

the fire in the centre of the floor and allow the smoke to escape as best it could. Of course, the ordinary fuel was wood, and wood smoke, though pungent, is not so dense as that of the modern coal fire. Still, there could be little of either cleanliness or comfort, according to our ideas, under such conditions. In such contemporary records, too, as Bishop Hall's account of the copyholder's cottage, the ' sluttish soote ' is the thing to which he draws particular attention, though, on the other hand, William Harrison makes a special plea for the healthiness of the smoke, reminding one rather of the solemn arguments of a heavy smoker as to the antiseptic qualities of tobacco fumes.

The first approach to a chimney is the canopy of wood and plaster which was erected over the great fire in the manorial hall, and so, probably, the first fireplaces were built, not against the wall, but in the middle of the room. In the case of the old lofty hall, which extended the whole height of the building, this would not cause any inconvenience, but complications would ensue if there were other rooms above. At Oughtbridge Hall, near Sheffield, a large central chimney-stack of stone from the kitchen passed right through the middle of a bedroom, rendering the room useless. This was obviously a later addition, as a piece had been cut out of the heavy ridge-tree, to make room for it. With the carelessness which you often find in old work, the cut ends of the beam were left without any support but the pins which attached them to the rafters. It seems to have been quite a common thing for the old chimneys to have cut into the room above, and their great size render possible the many old tales of a room in the chimney.

At so late a date as 1538, the central cover carried straight up to the roof seems to have been the usual method, for in that year Leland, writing about his visit to Bolton Castle, expresses wonder that the flues were carried up the walls. ' One thinge I muche noted in the haulle of Bolton, how chimneys were conveyed by tunnels made in the syds of the wauls, betwyxt the lights in the haulle ; and by this means, and by no covers, is the smoke of the harthe wonder strangely conveyed.'

But there was one danger ever present with the dwellers in wooden houses, which in our day we hardly realise ; the danger of fire. The old houses burnt like tinder, and when the fire lay open on the hearth and rushes strewed the floor, it would be the easiest thing in the world for a stray spark to set the whole place alight. The introduction of chimneys would almost be an aggravation of the evil, as the flue would soon collect a coating of soot where sparks could smoulder till they reached the laths which, with plaster, composed the chimney. Such a fire once started, from its position up in the wall and near the roof, would soon get a hold of the very fabric of the building, and be almost impossible to put out. And there is another danger still—sparks might drop from the chimney on to the thatch.

So from a very early date, indeed from the time that bricks came into common use in the fifteenth century, you find everywhere the corporations making bye-laws to guard against this danger. Thatch is whitewashed, chimneys are built higher, and, most important of all, wood is strictly forbidden in their construction. The earlier chimneys had sometimes been made of wickerwork, and even now there survive in Surrey and Sussex some curious examples of chimneys in wattle and clay, others were of lath and plaster, but soon brick became the chief and almost the only material in use.

In the court-leet of the Borough of Clare, Suffolk, is an entry dated 17th August 1621, ordering 'John Skinner of Sudbury, who has a dangerous chimney, to amend it.' Then comes the following: 'Item. We, the chief inhabitants and headboroughs of Clare, at the present court assembled, doe for ever hereafter, for the good estate of the towne, doe conclude, order, and agree, that no man shall erect, and build up any chimney within the borough, but only of bricke, and to be builded abov the roof of the house fower feete and a halfe, upon the paine for every such offence to be hereafter committed the summe of V*l*.' On the 9th October of the same year is an entry: 'John Skinner fined Xs. for not amending his chimney as ordered.' But the town of Clare seems to have a lot of trouble with its chimneys, for a hundred years later, we have an entry of much the same sort: 1719, April 7th: 'Item. We present Mr. Jno. Smith, clay chimney, and Mrs. Grace Lugdens, clay chimney, and ye Town House chimney where Jno. Martin live, if not all made new brick chimneys, within 3 months, do fine them 10s. a piece.'

And we may suppose that other towns passed similar bye-laws.

It was probably not until the second half of the sixteenth century that chimneys in the smaller dwellings became common. At that time they were added to many houses, and were simply built on to the out-

side of the house. These outside chimneys form
a conspicuous feature in many old cottages, and
their decorative qualities led to their often being
built with new cottages as well as merely added to the
old. Built clear of the walls, their broad base has
ample space not only for the wide, old-fashioned wood-
fire, but for the ingle-nook often lit by a little window
in the chimney wall.

Very beautiful in general proportions these old
chimneys were, so massive below, so slender above,
and the transition from the broad base to the narrow
shaft afforded opportunity for charming and graceful
decoration. Sometimes it tapered in a simple slope,
which was covered with tiles; at other times it went
up in a series of crow-steps, each with a little ornamental cap. But it is difficult to find an example
unmutilated, as the cap is easily displaced, and in
most cases has been lost.

Cosy as the ingle-nooks were, they must often have
been very uncomfortable to sit in, as the huge fireplace
with the capacious chimney was apt to smoke very
badly. Nowadays, one finds a little curtain hanging
from the huge oak beam which spans the fireplace,
which to some extent abates the nuisance. Another
device was to let the wood ash accumulate on the open

hearth until the fire itself was burning a foot or two above the floor-level. Often the iron dogs that supported the logs were of local workmanship, as were the boldly executed cast-iron firebacks, which now find their way into the antique shops.

As time went on, the more common form of chimney was that built in the wall itself.

Another form, however, is seen, especially in Surrey, where it is used with fine decorative effect as in the plate facing page 278.[1] Here all the chimney-stacks are grouped together and brought up in the centre of the roof. One advantage of this style of building the chimneys was, that it rendered the cottage very warm.

Like the roofs, these chimneys owe their pleasing effect to two causes, first, their fine proportions, and second, the loving care which has been lavished on every detail. The cottages of Surrey, especially in the Haselmere district, are particularly marked by the elegance of their chimneys, as may be seen in the example just mentioned. Much of the effect is due to the skilful grouping of the flues, which form, not a square block, but a collection of joined shafts with many angles, and thus give a variety of light and shade. The head of each shaft in the finer examples

1. Plate 63 in this edition

is formed of projecting courses of bricks; sometimes these are specially moulded, but delightful results are obtained by the use of the ordinary brick. A course of brick also projects at the bottom, and as the object is to carry off rain-water, it occurs just above the junction of the chimney and the roof, and is therefore at a different level at the sides from the front. The bricks used in the old work are thinner than used nowadays, and the same chimneys built in modern brick would look heavy and clumsy.

The old chimneys had no pots, though these doubtless add much to the utility of the chimney, and do not as a rule detract from its appearance when they have been added, as they now have in most cases. Sometimes old chimneys were built closed at the top, with side openings to allow the smoke to escape, a device with the same object as our whirligigs, old wives, and eccentric chimney-pots, and one often sees a sort of hood built with brick above the chimney as a protection from down-draughts.

Almost as important, as far as comfort is concerned, as the evolution of the chimneys, is that of the glazed window as we know it to-day. Originally windows were mere apertures in the wall, as may be seen from the name, wind-eye or wind-hole, and naturally they were kept as small as possible. Until the sixteenth century glass windows, except in churches and gentlemen's houses, were extremely rare. They were considered not as part of the house-fittings, but as movable property, and were so dealt with in wills. Noblemen travelling from one of their country-seats to another had the casements detachable, and carried them with them.

Poorer people, instead of glass, had open lattice-work, or framed blinds of cloth or canvas, called ' Fenestrals.' In the time of Henry VIII., linen dipped in oil was extensively used, and would have some degree of transparency ; and even a hundred years later, the cottages in the more remote parts of the country were no better off.

But in the sixteenth century glass became much cheaper. It found its way into the little cottages where it had not been known before, and in gentlemen's houses it became the fashion to have the windows as large as possible. In some cases the craze for glass was, no doubt, carried too far, and Lord Bacon's grumble that you could not tell whether you were inside or outside the house had some justification. Sometimes practically the whole timber-framing would be filled with glass. We hear of

' Hardwick Hall, more glass than wall,' and may still see a window in great Tangley Manor with ten lights in a row. But there can be no doubt the increased light thus introduced into the houses was greatly to the advantage of the inmates as regards health.

It is a safe general rule that the smaller the windows the older the house. The old bedroom windows were tiny things nestling under the eaves, and so low that they were little use for either lighting or ventilation.

It is interesting to note the evolution of the dormer window (*i.e.* bedroom window) from this primitive form.

The first improvement was an obvious one, namely to heighten the window by cutting a piece out of the roof. The first dormers were raised comparatively little above the line of the eaves, and the thatch merely took a curve over them, the roof being as before all one surface. When tiles took the place of thatch, a different treatment was necessary, and the earliest plan may be seen in the plate facing page 72,[1] where a strip of the main roof, so to speak, is lifted up to cover the top of the dormer, and the sides of the window are made up of a little wall supporting this roof.

The next step is when the dormer gets a ridge-roof of its own, as in the plate facing page 104,[2] and once this

1. Plate 16 in this edition
2. Plate 23

stage is reached, it is but a step to inserting a small gable with the window in the centre, and this grows till in some cases it is higher than the main roof, for the constant tendency was for windows to grow larger and rooms more airy.

A reaction occurred later, when people began to build up windows owing to the imposition of the window-tax, surely one of the most inane and one of the most iniquitous pieces of legislation ever devised.

This tax continued in existence for a period of over a hundred and fifty years, and excited, justly too, more discontent and ill-feeling than almost any other imposition.

It first came in the treacherous guise of a blessing. In 1662, after the Restoration, money was urgently wanted by Charles II., and a house-tax was imposed, formed on the model of a French one, a charge being levied on every hearth or stove in the house. The tax was known as hearth-money or chimney-money, and the visits of the chimney men, as they were called, were resented and resisted as invasions of the English home. So fierce was the opposition that the tax was repealed, and in 1696 a new house-tax imposed, and in this case the rate was calculated not on the hearths, but on the windows, which, it was plausibly argued, could be counted from the outside without the need of disturbing the householder.

And this time the tax had come to stay. All through the eighteenth century it continued, rising higher and higher during the French wars. It was interpreted harshly too. 'Window,' said the judge, meant 'wind-eye' or wind-hole, and any aperture that let in light or air was a window. As the bitter doggerel rhyme of the day said:

'We'll tell them we pay for the light of the sun,
    For the flash of a candle to cheer the dark night,
    For a hole in the wall if it let in the light.'

It is difficult to estimate the evil done by such legislation. Householders blocked up windows wholesale, and new buildings were built with fewer and fewer. In Edinburgh, it was said that a row of houses was built without a window in the bedroom floor.

In spite of repeated parliamentary discussions, it was not till 1851 that the Act was removed from the statute-book.

Some old cottages have the upper windows set forward on brackets. Not only has this a good effect, but it enlarges the room and allows for a large window-board. Beautiful examples of this style of window may be seen at Orpington, at Canterbury, Tonbridge, and other places, but they do not appear to have been anywhere very common, and occur much more often in towns than in the country.

In the oldest houses the windows were fitted into the frame of the house, as may be seen in the gable-window of the plate facing page 146, and the jambs, sills, and heads worked on the solid posts. In later work, however, these were cut away and frames inserted. The window-frames were generally moulded, invariably so in the older cottages. Now and again, one finds windows with stone heads and sides, and even stone mullions, but though common in farmhouses and manors, they are not so common in the smaller houses.

The glazing of the old windows is one of their chief beauties. They were invariably filled with small leads. The oldest shape for the glass quarries seems to have been not the well-known diamond pane, but a square ; but after the diagonal style appeared, it became much more common than the other. The old diamond panes are a much prettier shape than modern imitations, being less elongated. Sometimes one finds a pane left unglazed, and filled with a pierced lead ventilator, cut into the most delightful patterns.

Unfortunately most of the old leaded lights are disappearing, and their place being taken by modern

1. Plate 33 in this edition

large paned windows. One cannot wonder at this for several reasons. In the first place, the old windows were often very badly fitted, though it may sound treason to say so to the ears of those who are accustomed to believe that everything that is old must be good. But so it is ; the leads are weak, and they often leak badly. Again, however picturesque they look from the outside, from within it must be confessed that they are rather irritating. Your view is obscured to a great extent by the leads, and the different colours that one finds in so many different panes are disturbing. And where the old glass is taken out, and the window repaired, the reglazing is almost invariably done in ordinary shaped panes, for the simple reason that the cost of the other is prohibitive. Such small leaded lights cost about five times as much as ordinary glazing, and more than the price of plate-glass.

In the illustrations to this volume, one of the few liberties which the artist has taken with her subjects is to carefully restore the old lattice-windows where they have been tampered with.

The doorways partake of the same character as the window mouldings. In the early examples—up to the end of the sixteenth century—they were of Gothic character, generally slightly arched, and with carving on the spandrils, and moulded jambs and stops. The Tudor arch may be seen in some of the old cottages illustrated, as in the plates facing pages 58 and 107.[1] Sometimes the original oak doors still remain. It is interesting to note that these are not usually panelled, but of match-boarding, nailed on battens. Formerly the old doors were adorned with finely wrought-iron hinges, and the latch, the keyhole, and the knocker were all things of beauty, and the window fastenings were equally interesting. Most of this old metal-work was tinned, giving it a fine colour.

If as it should be, the interior of the old cottage is just what one would expect from the exterior. Spotlessly clean, it presents a combination of neatness and comfort, which makes even poverty seem attractive, and has made the idyllic picture of ' Love in a Cottage ' the very perfection of domestic felicity. Certainly from the outside the picture is very charming in its simplicity, and the little inconveniences that arise in actual experience are not evident to the passing visitor.

The rooms are low, seldom more than eight feet high, but then ' Heaven's gates are not so highly arched as princes' palaces.' And the low room, with

1. Plates 14 and 24 in this edition

the big oak beams running across the ceiling, looks very cosy. In the oldest examples these beams are moulded with deeply cut hollows and headings, but, as elsewhere, these details die out in the later work.

The kitchen, in the smaller cottages, is, of course, living-room and kitchen combined, and its chief feature is the large open fireplace, generally spanned by a huge oak beam. Above the mantel-piece runs a rack for the long, bright spits used with the wood-fires, and sometimes the elaborate clock-work apparatus, for turning the spit, is still to be seen. The old oak dresser, bright with its china and pewter, the latter all too rare now, is the best furniture for the kitchen, and with the well-scrubbed table and wooden chairs, just fit in with the general scheme. Sometimes you get a bit of bright brass and copper; candlesticks, or warming-pans, that catch the fire-light and bring dancing lights across the room, and in the open window are sweet-smelling flowers. But nowadays, alas, one seldom finds a cottage in this unspoilt condition.

The floor has sometimes its original paving of irregularly shaped pieces of flat stone, a fancy often continued outside the cottage door, as seen in the plate facing the next page. The modern papers, which have covered up the wall surface, must take away a good deal of the original appearance of the cottage interior; but the quaint coloured pictures which one used to see, though modern reproductions and photographs are fast displacing them, are quite in keeping with their surroundings. In the old days, as we may see from Harrison's pages, the plastered walls in the better-class houses were hung with tapestries and other cloths.

' In plastering, likewise, of our fairest houses over our heads,' he says, ' we use to laie first a laire or two of white mortar tempered with haire, upon lathes, which are nailed one by another (or sometimes upon reed or wickers, more dangerous for fire, and made fast here and there with sap lathes for falling downe), and finallie cover all with the aforesaid plaster, which, beside the delectable whitenesse of the stuffe it selfe, is laced on so even and smoothlie as nothing, in my judgement, can be done with more exactnesse. The walls of our houses on the inner sides, in like sort, be either hanged with tapesteries, arras worke, or painted cloths, where in either diverse histories or hearbes, beasts, knots, and such like are stained, or else they are sieled with oke of our own or waine-scot brought hither out of the east countries, where

by the rooms are not a little commended, made warm
and much more close than otherwise they would be.'

The stair which leads to the upper rooms was not
built in modern form with balustrades until the
seventeenth century, the primitive form being
merely a ladder from the living-room to the bedroom
above. Another old form runs round a central post,
like the stair in church-towers. In very old cottages,
the upper bedrooms, with the windows away down
under the eaves, are little better than garrets, badly
ventilated, and badly lit, the windows are so low.
In no place but the centre of the room can one stand
upright, and in very primitive dwellings one finds
only this central part floored, and no plaster ceiling
at all, only the bare rafters overhead.

But in the later and better-class cottages, the dormer
and gabled windows make these rooms much more
comfortable and healthy. The fireplaces in the
upper rooms have, in the better-class houses, a Tudor
arch of brick, but in the smaller ones an oak beam
is used as before. Sometimes an oak fender curb
remains ; the hearth in that case is sometimes made
level with the top of the curb, and lies on the top
of the beams and joists; at other times these are cut
into, to admit the hearth flush with the floor.

In very few cases do the old cottages stand now as originally built, but have been added to and altered as time went on. This, indeed, is one of their greatest charms—the unstudied way in which they have expanded in whatever direction utility required. It almost seems a natural growth, and after a few years, what was a new addition is toned and mellowed into harmony with the rest.

And the older the building, the less likelihood of finding it in the original condition.

Sometimes we find a new casing built round a fifteenth-century framework, which is thus quite hidden and only discovered when the building is pulled down. In the larger fifteenth-century farmhouses and manors, what was originally the old lofty hall has generally been converted into two stories by the insertion of a floor half-way up, thus forming dining room below and bedrooms above. Often too, in Elizabeth's time, a gable wing, or wings, was added to an old central structure. As we have seen, most pre-Elizabethan cottages had no chimneys, and these have been added as occasion required, and often a lean-to has a little chimney of its own.

Changes in the roofing material, too, have taken place. Thatch in many places has given place to

tile, though I am of the opinion that many tiled roofs
date right back to Elizabethan times. Still, where
one finds a high-pitched roof covered with tiles, the
likelihood is that it was originally thatched. If the
change has taken place quite within recent years,
the shape of the machine-made tile will show this ;
but if a hand-made tile has been used, it soon
acquires a mellow and beautiful appearance. Horsham
slabs, too, are superseded by tiles in the same
way.

But these alterations, more or less ancient, add to,
rather than take away from the beauty of the
buildings.

It is only when the modern contractor proceeds to
restore a building, to ' do it up,' as the process is termed,
that we find havoc played with its finer features.
And the sins of the modern restorer are many. When
he supplies tiles, they are of the machine-made order,
often with a patent surface that resists the gentle
action of the weather, which stains the old tile with
mossy greens and gold, and they are laid in lines of
mathematical straightness. Often too, instead of the
tile, he puts on a hideous, thin purple slate, of the style
so detested by William Morris.

Then he loses the elegant lines of the framework

by facing the building with brick, or he covers the whole structure with a sheathing of cement. In addition to losing the original surface, by these means he sets back the windows in relation to the wall surface.

The windows themselves often come in for alteration, and we must admit that the old tiny windows are more picturesque from the outside than comfortable or healthy for the dwellers within. But it is heartbreaking to see the old timbers of the frame sawed through wantonly, to admit the larger windows, when a little ingenuity in placing the window would have resulted in just as much convenience, without damage to the structure. The new windows, too, are often cheap American frames, which ill replace the beautiful old casements.

The chimney also is a feature which comes in for a good deal of alteration, for elegant though these are, it must be confessed that they usually smoked pretty badly, and so sometimes the stacks are heightened, or bare, hideous cowls added.

The old oak timbers which weather to such a clear silvery grey are now often blackened with tar, following a fashion which seems to have originated in the north, and is not more than one hundred years old.

PLATE 25. OLD FARM NEAR DOWNTON, WILTS.

PLATE 26. NEAR ALDERLEY EDGE, CHESHIRE

PLATE 27. AT HAGBOURNE, BERKS.

PLATE 28. HARVEST FIELD NEAR WESTERHAM, KENT

PLATE 29. DOWNS NEAR WESTERHAM, KENT

PLATE 30. BLUEBELL WOOD, KENT

PLATE 31. VILLAGE STREET, KENT

PLATE 32. FEEDING THE FOWLS

The idea is to preserve them, in most cases a precaution quite unnecessary, as they are as hard as iron. Still, this is better than the sham timber frame fixed to the front of new buildings in imitation of the old.

CHAPTER VII

THE COTTAGES OF KENT AND SURREY

'A Knight of Cales, a Gentleman of Wales,
And a Laird of the north countrie.
A yeoman of Kent with his yearly rent
Will buy them out all three.'

OLD SAYING.

OF all parts of England none is richer in old cottage buildings, and indeed in antiquities generally, than the south-eastern corner formed of the counties of Kent, Surrey, and Sussex. For in the early days this was the most important and the wealthiest district in the country.

Many circumstances combined to give it this pre-eminence, but most important of all was its position facing the narrow seas. Here was the point of com-munication between the island and the mainland. On this strip of coast landed the successive invasions of England, Romans, Saxons, and Normans, and here in times of peace the stream of traffic poured back and forward between England and France.

From the earliest times the little havens along the

coast, from the Medway on the east to Beachy Head in the west, were the centres of a busy trade. Each one of them had its fleet of smacks manned by hardy crews, who were fishermen, traders, privateersmen, or pirates as occasion served. These became a sort of police, guarding our frontier coast, and in time their services to the country at large were recognised, and the defence of the Channel entrusted to them. Banded together in the association of the Cinque Ports, they guaranteed a certain number of ships and men for this purpose, and in return received many privileges, including immunity from national taxation, and almost complete self-government, so that the burghers of the seaside towns waxed fat and prosperous, and their ships formed the first English navy. Seaworthy their vessels must have been, though small, and they expert seamen, for their favourite plan of battle was to bear down on the enemy during a gale.

From each of these seaport towns a road ran inland converging on the market-town of Canterbury, distant about a day's march, which thus served as a depot for the continental trade. From Canterbury, too, ran the great path to the west, which brought the produce of the mines of Cornwall, and which, later on, when Canterbury had its cathedral, and the cathedral the shrine of a martyr, was known as the Pilgrims' Way. But it is much older than Chaucer's pilgrims, and probably older than the days of the Romans. So Canterbury was a wealthy and important town, the headquarters of the English Church, a busy trade depot, and the centre of the richest agricultural land of England.

For Kent has always been the garden of England. The Weald, indeed, in those days was part of one huge forest, extending into Surrey and Sussex, where huge herds of pigs were turned in to feed on the acorns which strewed the ground, but along by the coast and in the south and east of the country were strips of fertile land.

From the time of its introduction into England, Kent has been the centre of the hop-growing industry, and there are those who maintain that the hops produced there are still the finest in the world.

When the output of hops reached its height in 1878, out of 72,000 acres for the whole country, Kent supplied 46,600 acres, and though the area under cultivation has been reduced of late years, in 1906 Kent had 29,296 acres out of a total of 46,722. And though the acreage has been less, the crop has not decreased, owing to the improved methods of cultivation. In the early part of the nineteenth century, 6 cwt. per acre was a fair yield ; for the five years, 1887-91, there were 35,953 acres, which yielded an average of 6·9 cwt. per acre, a total of 248,075 cwt. ; while for 1902-6, while the acreage had sunk to 29,875, the average was 9 cwt. per acre, yielding a crop of 268,875 cwt.

In 1905 the Kentish hops produced 14½ cwt., but so fickle are the harvests that the crop of 1906 only averaged 6 cwt. At present, therefore, hops are one of the most speculative crops grown. They require the most skilful farming, and at times an attack of insects or fungoid growths may necessitate great expense in spraying and otherwise treating the plants, to save the crop. They require a great deal of manual labour in digging up the soil, the manuring is most costly, and the labour of erecting the complicated system of poling is very great. Formerly the hops were trained upon temporary poles, but nowadays more permanent arrangements of wire fixed to stout posts are found more satisfactory, though less picturesque. From posts to wire is threaded a network of string of coarse nut fibre, which is renewed each year, and various methods of stringing are used in different parts.

Picking the crop begins in September and lasts for some weeks, during which time from 45,000 to 65,000 of the scum of London are let loose in the hop-fields. Special trains bring them down in the early morning, and they can earn from four to five shillings per day. After picking, the hops are dried in the oast-houses, and then packed in 'pockets' of one and a half hundredweight.

Like a backbone the ridge of the north downs cuts across the country, its rounded outlines broken here and there by a white crescent, where an old chalk quarry has eaten into the hillside. Along this southern slope, about half-way up, and three hundred feet above the plain, runs the Pilgrims' Way. Times have changed much since the pilgrims used that path. Then the land below was largely waste forest and marsh, and it was a dangerous adventure to leave the open highway and strike off through the woodlands. But above the path was dry underfoot, and clear and free from ambush.

But now, if we look from the high ground over the plain below, it is a changed scene. In the distance, indeed, the Weald, rising low ridge behind low ridge—

for it seems to run like the sea in a series of billows—melts into a blue haze, just as it must always have done on a summer's day, but it is a different landscape near at hand since Chaucer's time. Fields upon fields of hops, the poles standing up in long, regular lines, while every here and there is a farm with its red-brick and red-tiled oast-houses. At whatever season you go, the hops dominate the Kentish landscape. In the spring there are the groves of bare poles, with the maze of cords crossing and recrossing, and in the summer these are wreathed with vine-like tendrils, a beautiful sight. In the autumn comes the clustered fruit, and in the winter the bare poles are stacked in the empty fields. And over it all, like watchful guardians, stand the oast-houses, their cowls turning this way and that with the wind, and giving an air of untiring vigilance.

Kent is well wooded, and of this woodland more than three-quarters is under coppice, for the growing of hop-poles is a most important industry. The county is full of little copses, which are allowed to grow several years, and then cut down to the stumps, to send forth new shoots. Those copses, probably from their open character, are particularly favoured by the bluebells, so that in early summer the green grass seems to reflect the blue sky. But it is a more changeable blue than that overhead, running from rich azures to the palest tints, and shot with delicate pinks and rich purples.

But this copsewood industry has declined of late years. Poles are being creosoted, which makes them last much longer, and the new permanent systems of poling have caused a demand for larger poles, so that the wood has to be allowed to grow for a longer period.

But though the most important, hops are not the only agricultural produce of Kent. As a fruit county it holds the foremost place in England, for in addition to the advantages of rich soil and warm climate, the proximity of London gives it a ready market, so that the fruit industry has grown steadily during the last thirty years.

The apple orchards are a lovely sight when all ablaze with pink blossom, and besides apples, we have pears, plums, greengages, cherries, adding to the beauty of the scene. The smaller fruits, too, strawberries, raspberries, currants, and gooseberries, are grown in large quantities, and Kent has always been famous as a nut district.

The county is very rich in fine old houses, and in

quaint old villages. In the illustration facing page 138,[1] we have a typical little village street, the long, irregular line of houses, the roofs of all shapes and varieties. It reminds one a little of Otford's straggling street, through which the Pilgrims' Way runs just after crossing the valley of the Darent. A sleepy little place is Otford, with its crooked line of crooked houses, and at the end the old church, with its squat, square tower. Every cottage is old, and the village inn, the Bull, has a fine stone fireplace taken from Otford Castle, now in ruins. There are beautiful old farmhouses near by, with sheds and barns less pretentious, but almost more beautiful than the red-brick house.

Following the Pilgrims' Way, we find, two miles further on, and lying some fifty yards below the road, the little village of Kemsing, with its sacred well, and a church where the pilgrims used to call. If you put your hand on the old oak door to push it open, you will find your fingers sink into a hollow some inches deep, worn by the hands of countless pilgrims, who have pushed that door open just as you do now.

Hidden among the trees on the ridge to the south lies Sevenoaks, where Jack Cade's Kentishmen defeated the royal forces in 1450—a fine town, with

1. Plate 31 in this edition

its old-fashioned High Street, and its cricket ground, claimed to be the oldest in England. Close by lies Knole Park. The house is one of the most extensive of all the great Elizabethan mansions, and the park has few equals in England. Of great extent, it is broken up into a series of ridges and valleys, the ridges well wooded, the valleys carpeted with green turf. The timber is magnificent. There are two great beeches, the one twenty-seven and a half, and the other twenty-eight feet in girth, and an oak which was known as ' the old oak ' in 1650. In the valleys, too, are hawthorns, some so old that they have fallen, and writhe and twist along the ground, still bearing every spring their clouds of white blossom.

The house would accommodate the population of a small town. The chimneys are tall and ornamented with moulded brick-work, and the series of leaden rain water-heads is well known to architects and craftsmen. Within the massive brick wall, which divides the precincts of the house from the park, is a fine old garden, with sundials and walks among lines of clipped yews. The park stands on high ground, which at the southern boundary drops suddenly into the Weald, and from the crest of a ridge one commands a splendid view of the surrounding country.

A few miles to the south lies Penshurst Place, once the seat of Sir Philip Sidney, an older house than Knole, and even more interesting. The old hall is still in its original condition, and when the fine oak roof was renewed recently, the oaks of the park supplied the necessary timber. In architecture the hall is early English, but the bulk of the house is Elizabethan. The old chimneys are particularly fine, and more richly ornamented than those of Knole.

The village of Penshurst is one of the most picturesque of all Kentish villages. The little square-towered church lies behind the village street, and you enter the churchyard through a passage which runs under one of the houses, the upper story of which is supported on massive oaken pillars. One of the gables facing the churchyard has a beautiful old cusped barge-board, and many of the cottages near are marked by some special feature. There are few prettier 'bits' than the view from the bridge over the river of the village street and church.

A mile or two away lies Chiddingstone, with its tiny street of some seven or eight cottages, all somewhere about three hundred years old. The wooden framework here has never been blacked, and shows the natural silver-grey of the old oak. The central house is specially well known, and has figured on many an artist's canvas—the porch-house, it is called, as it has a projecting square porch, supported on huge pillars of oak. Inside, the walls are covered with oak-panelling richly carved. In a field behind the village lies a huge boulder, the 'chiding stone,' from which the village takes its name. It is supposed to have done duty as a pillory, the culprit being chained to the top of it, and exposed to the derision of the public.

Not far off is Ightham, another beautiful old village, right in the midst of the nut district. These Kentish cobs, as they are called, grow on little bushes, not much bigger than gooseberry bushes, and may be here seen in fields. Apple orchards too abound, planted in regular rows, which with their white-washed stems have a peculiarly military appearance. Not in the village of Ightham itself, but near by, is one of the finest old houses in the county, Ightham Mote, the very model of an old moated grange, and worthy to compare with the finest old halls of Cheshire and Lancashire.

And all this is within a diameter of some eight miles. One might go all over the country, and find similar features of interest in every district. Numberless quaint villages and many old-fashioned towns, such as Westerham, so loved by Jane Austen, and full of fine Georgian houses, and Tunbridge Wells, with its Pantiles, once the rival of Bath.

The natural features of Surrey differ a little from those of Kent. It is less an agricultural district, being very thickly wooded. From the banks of the Thames southward stretched a thick forest which, in the days when charcoal was consumed on the domestic hearth, supplied the city with fuel. Croydon was the centre of the charcoal district, for in 1568, out of twenty-four Surrey colliers who were summoned before the Court of Exchequer on a charge of supplying sacks which were light weight, twenty came from Croydon, the rest from Waddon, Sutton, and Carshalton. This natural forest was the basis of many of the industries of the county, for charcoal then supplied the place of coal now, and manufactories naturally clustered round the edge of the forest land.

In the south of the county, too, occurs the geological formation known as the 'Hastings sand,' which is suitable for glass-making; and at Chiddingfold we have the first glass-works which were established in England, there being mention of glass made there as far back as 1230. In 1351 John Allemagne of Chiddingfold supplied glass for the windows of St. Stephen's Chapel, Westminster. The industry continued to flourish till the beginning of the seventeenth century, though the quality of the glass made did not seem to compare favourably with that imported from abroad. The following very laudatory notice, however, which occurs in Charnock's *Breviary*, published in 1577, would rather lead one to suppose the contrary:

> ' As for glass-makers they be scant in this land,
> Yet one there is as I doe understand :
> And in Sussex (*sic*) is now his habitacion,
> At Chiddinsfold he works of his occupacion :
> To go to town it is necessary and meete,
> Or send a servant that is discrete :
> And desire him in most humble wise
> To blow thee a glasse after thy devise :
> It were worth many an Arme or a Legg
> He could shape it like to an egge
> To open and to close as close as a haire,
> If thou hast such a one thou needst not feare :
> Yet if thou hadst a number in to store
> It is the better for store is no sore.'

The royal proclamation of 1615, prohibiting entirely the use of charcoal as a fuel in glass-making, dealt a death-blow to the Chiddingfold glass industry, though the prosperity of the district was still maintained by cloth-making and tanning.

The iron works of the Weald formed another Surrey

industry which depended on the charcoal of the forest for its fuel, but this industry was not either of such great antiquity or of such importance as the ironworks of Sussex of which fuller mention is made in the next chapter.

Guildford, Godalming, and Farnham were the centres of a great woollen cloth industry which flourished in the southern parts of the county, and reached the height of its prosperity in the sixteenth and seventeenth centuries, and contributed not a little to the wealth of the district.

But one of the most notable industries had its seat in the beautiful little valley which runs west from Guildford towards Dorking. Early in the seventeenth century, the Chilworth Gunpowder-Mills were established by the banks of the little stream there, so that in the words of an old writer, 'this little romancy vale' became 'a little black commonwealth of powder-makers who were as black as negroes.' Sometimes the valley was shaken with terrible explosions, for the same old writer records that five mills were blown up in less than a year, and a mill below Shere once sent a piece of timber flying through an adjoining cottage, which took off the head of a woman as she sat at her spinning-wheel. But the industry still continues, and the Chilworth Mills are still among the most important in the kingdom. Besides the powder-mills in the valley, there are paper-mills, both of which are vigorously condemned by William Cobbett in a passage as remarkable for its beautiful English as for its perverse reasoning.

' This pretty valley of Chilworth has a run of water which comes out of the high hills, and which, occasionally, spreads into a pond ; so that there is, in fact, a series of ponds connected by this run of water. This valley, which seems to have been created by Providence as one of the choicest retreats of man, which seems formed for a scene of innocence and happiness, has been, by ungrateful man, so perverted as to make it instrumental in effecting two of the most damnable of purposes ; in carrying into execution two of the most damnable inventions that ever sprung from the mind of man under the influence of the devil !—namely, the making of gunpowder and of bank-notes ! Here, in this tranquil spot, where the nightingales are to be heard earlier and later than in any other part of England ; where the first bursting of the buds is seen in opening ; where no rigour of seasons can ever be felt ; where everything seems formed for precluding the very thought of wickedness ; here has the devil fixed

on as one of the seats of his grand manufactory :
and perverse and ungrateful man not only lends him
his aid, but lends it cheerfully. As to the gunpowder,
indeed, we might get over that. In some cases that
may be innocently, and, when it sends the lead at the
hordes that support a tyrant, meritoriously employed.
The alders and the willows, therefore, one can see,
without so much regret, turned into powder by the
waters of this valley. But the bank-notes! To
think that the springs which God has commanded to
flow from the sides of these happy hills, for the comfort
and delight of man—to think that these springs should
ever be perverted into means of spreading misery over
a whole nation.'

And the valley is full of fine old buildings. Shere
is a spot beloved by artists, who frequent its fine old
inn, and have left many souvenirs of their visit in
the albums of the landlord. Albury and Gomshall,
too, are full of beauty spots, the former possessing
a little inn with the most elaborate chimneys I ever
saw in so small a building.

It is evident then, that with so many sources of
wealth, Surrey must be rich in old buildings, and so
it is. Some of the most beautiful specimens which
survive are found in this county, of which we may

mention Great Tangley Manor, perhaps the best example of an ornamental timber house in the south, and Crowhurst Place, dating from the fifteenth century, and a very fine specimen of the early manor-house.

But in this volume we are more concerned with the humbler dwellings. These, too, are affected by the general wealth of the district, and are at once roomier, more elaborate in design, and generally more important than we find elsewhere except in Kent. The cottages of the two counties, indeed, have many features in common. The abundant use of brick, the prevalence of tiled roofs, rather than thatch, the use of weather-tiles, and the elegant and elaborate chimneys.

Particularly fine are the cottages in the southern part of Surrey round about Haslemere.

There could not be a better example of the old English cottage than that facing this page.[1] The cottage large and roomy, the beautiful frame of timber showing clearly, the chimneys massed on the ridge, while the kitchen chimney has a separate stack to itself by the side. Many features are noteworthy. The elegant treatment of the gabled wing—note that its roof is slightly higher than the main roof—and the curious arrangement of small, broken roofs which run down to the ground on the other side. The window, too,

1. Plate 33 in this edition

in the gable is framed by the solid beams of the structure, as is the little window under the eaves. The frame, as is usual in Surrey and Kent, is filled in with brick. Another example of a similar nature may be seen in the plate facing page 142.[1] In this case the bricks have been plastered over, and this plaster scaling off, and showing the clear red in patches, has a charming effect.

The example facing page 278[2] is even more interesting, as it embodies a unique type prevalent only in this neighbourhood. The tall, graceful chimneys, with their delicately moulded tops, the steep roof with hip at each end (and in this case beautified by lichen of grey and gold), the rich and ornate weather-tiling, the compactness and simplicity of the whole plan, its elegance arising from beauty of proportion and careful finish in each detail ;—all these things mark the best examples from the Haslemere district.

Another example may be seen in the plate facing page 72.[3] The roof here is even steeper in pitch, and the chimneys, right in the centre, tower up with a very imposing effect. But in spite of the slight extra height added to the room by dormer windows, it is evident that the rooms under the roof in such a cottage must be inconvenient and dark, and in the

1. Plate 32 in this edition
2. Plate 63
3. Plate 16

roof itself there is a great waste of space. But whatever fault we may find with its utility, there is no doubt as to the fine appearance of those high-pitched roofs. They give an air of distinction and completeness to the cottage which places them apart, and makes other styles look rambling and careless.

CHAPTER VIII

THE COTTAGES OF SUSSEX AND WESSEX

'Unnumbered cottages and farms,
That have, to musing minds, unnumbered charms.'
CRABBE.

As compared with Surrey and Kent, Sussex is, and appears always to have been, a poorer county and less well populated. Along the shore, indeed, were found prosperous and busy towns, of which Rye and Winchelsea were the chief, but inland the country was covered with forest, or with great open downs. The forest, indeed, stretched from the borders of Kent right down to Hampshire, a distance of one hundred and twenty miles. The forest of Anderida the Romans called it; Ashdown forest we call what little of it remains.

The most important industry of the county, the iron industry, was due to two factors, the presence of this abundant supply of wood, and of a geological formation, 'the Hastings sand' it was called, containing a large quantity of iron. From very early times the

Sussex iron industry was one of the most important in the county, much older and of greater extent than that of the adjoining counties, Surrey and Kent, and was the chief means of bringing wealth to the district.

Ironworks in the old days were very different from the huge establishments which we have to-day, and a short account of the methods used in the Sussex works at the time of their greatest development may be interesting.

After the ore was dug up, it was subjected to a preliminary firing, alternate layers of charcoal and ore being laid in a small kiln, and burnt sufficiently to allow the ore to be easily broken, but not enough to cause it to melt and run together. It was then taken to the furnace, which was a building some twenty-four feet square, and about thirty feet in height, containing an egg-shaped cavity, at the bottom of which was a hearth of sandstone, and the iron vent of the bellows. The last were worked at first by foot-blast, but in the middle of the sixteenth century, water-power was substituted. Once lit, the furnace was kept burning a long time, sometimes as long as forty weeks at a stretch. The heat increased gradually, and reached its maximum about ten weeks after it was lighted. During each 'foun-day' (working week of six days), on an average, eight tons of iron were produced at the expense of twenty-four loads of charcoal (each load eleven quarters), and as many loads of ore (eighteen bushels to the load). The ore, or mine, as it was termed, was cast in from above, and slowly melting, fell through into the hearth, from which it was run out into rough moulds of sand. The resulting mass of metal was called a sow if over one thousand pounds, a pig if less. The intense heat of the furnace gradually ate away the sandstone hearth, so that one which only turned out a pig of seven or eight hundred pounds, after a period of use was so much larger, that the pig had grown to a sow of two thousand pounds weight. The hearth had to be renewed at the end of every period of blowing.

The next step was working the iron at the forge. Here we had a large hammer of some seven or eight hundredweight worked by a water-wheel, and the iron was forged into bars as the most convenient form for disposal. Sometimes the bars were of a special size, suitable to be beaten into ploughshares.

It was in Henry VIII.'s reign that the Sussex iron-works became prominent, and from that time, until the introduction of coal fuel in the eighteenth century, they flourished exceedingly. In the sixteenth century they were largely employed in the manufacture of ordnance. At Lord Admiral Seymour's iron-mills in Worth forest alone, fifty-six tons one hundredweight of ordnance 'of dyvers sorts,' valued at £560, 15s., as well as fifty-two tons five hundredweight of shot for the same, were turned out between 1547 and January 1549. These were sent to the Tower, but it was whispered that guns made in Sussex found their way into even the hands of Spain, England's bitterest enemy in those days.

Pevensey was the chief port for the export of Sussex iron, and did a busy trade. But during the eighteenth century the iron industry shifted to the coal-fields of the north, and by 1740 there were only ten furnaces in Sussex. The last furnace was blown out in 1811, and the last forge closed in 1822.

But though the prosperity of the iron industry made the fortunes of many county families, and studded the district with many fine old mansion-houses, the type of the smaller buildings, the farm-houses and cottages, is poorer and more rural than in Surrey and Kent. We begin to get away from the influences of London into a more secluded country where the resources are smaller, and the type of the people more simple.

The oldest and most interesting houses are found in the little towns along the southern shore. Rye is famous for its quaint streets and old houses, and possesses two fine old fifteenth-century inns, the Mermaid and the Old Flushing Inn, while at Alfriston is another old inn, the Star, of the same period, with three picturesque oriel windows. Alfriston indeed, situated in a little valley of the Downs near Beachey Head, is rich in old buildings, including a timber-built and thatched clergy-house, which dates from the latter part of the fourteenth century. It contains a central hall with a fine open-timbered roof and a hooded fireplace, having end wings of two stories, in which were the parlour, buttery-hatch, and sleeping-rooms.

In Pevensey are several excellent examples of the sixteenth century, and a very interesting old house, dating from a much earlier period, is situated just at the Castle entrance. In early times it was the seat of the Mint, and the minting-chamber, with its great chimney-shaft, may still be seen. In the sixteenth century it was the home of Andrew Boorde (Merry Andrew), who had the house renewed and largely rebuilt, and it is said that he here entertained King Edward VI. One of the rooms is covered with richly carved oak-panelling of the fifteenth century, which until recently was hidden behind a facing of plaster, while, in several of the upper rooms, delicate frescoes have been discovered on the walls, dating from the same period. These are only now being exposed, being covered with many layers of white-wash, to which, doubtless, they owe their preservation. The house is in excellent condition, and is now used as a depot for the sale of old furniture, and the various rooms are open to visitors at a small charge.

A particularly fine example of the fifteenth century, as already pointed out, is the house at West Tarring, near Worthing, illustrated in the plate facing this page. It is noticeable that we find the oldest examples, as a rule, in the streets of towns or villages, and not standing isolated. Not only in this case are they much less exposed to the ravages of the weather, but the fact that any interference with them would largely affect the adjoining property, has allowed them to remain undisturbed, when often in these days of vandalism they would otherwise have been pulled down.

We have here the overhanging story supported

on a huge oak beam, and the narrow spacing of the posts. All the timber-work is interesting ; the massive beam above the window in the gable, the curved strut supporting the overhanging part of the roof, where it covers the recess of the second doorway, and the cusped and traceried barge-boards. All these are signs of an early date, and it is noticeable also that the quarries of the casement windows in the centre are not of the usual diamond shape, but are square, the older form of the two. The roof is a magnificent specimen of the use of Horsham slabs, and its low pitch, as compared with a thatched or tiled roof, is due to the greater weight of the stone.

One chief characteristic of the Sussex cottages is that brick and tile are so little used for the ' healing ' of roofs, thatch being the material chiefly employed. In the western parts reed thatch is largely used, but the most characteristic roofing material is the Horsham stone slate, a product of the neighbourhood. It has a fine appearance, and is practically indistructible, its chief defect being that, owing to its weight, it necessitates a low-pitched roof, which is not always water-tight.

A very characteristic style of Sussex, and, indeed, of all the chalk district, is the use of nodules of flint embedded in mortar. These are found in all buildings, from churches to cottages, combined with stonework or brick, or in some cases with timber-work. Sometimes the nodules are left in the rough, sometimes the exposed faces are squared. The same style of building is used for boundary walls, a coping of brick being added, and often a strengthening course at intervals.

From Sussex we pass into the great Wessex district, and into a country still more sequestered and rural. Far from the capital, there was little influx of wealth from that quarter, there were few industries, and the soil for the most part is poorer than in the east. But still we find here much that is most typical of England, and Nathaniel Hawthorne, in his English notes, writes thus of the country round Salisbury :

' I think I never saw such continued sylvan beauty as the road showed us, passing through a good deal of woodland—fine old trees standing each within its own space, and thus having full liberty to outspread itself and wax strong and broad for ages, instead of being crowded, and thus stifled and emaciated, as human beings are here, and forest trees in America. Hedges too, and the rich, rich verdure of England, and villages full of picturesque old houses, thatched and ivied, or perhaps overgrown with roses—a stately mansion in the Elizabethan style ; and a quiet stream gliding onward without a ripple from its own motion, but rippled by a large fish darting across it ; and over all this scene, a gentle, friendly sunshine, not ardent enough to crush a single leaf or blade of grass. Nor must the village church be forgotten, with its square, battlemented tower, dating back to the epoch of the Normans.'

There are few more interesting old English towns, indeed, than Salisbury. It is dominated by the cathedral, whose cool grey spire, exquisite in proportion, soars up into the clouds. From every direction this is the focus of our gaze ; you see it from far off on the high ground to the north, and it is reflected from the quiet waters of the river. When one approaches nearer to the great building, the huddled streets of the town fall back, as it were, to give it room, and there it stands on a beautiful level of soft green turf, the most perfect of all English cathedrals. Round the smooth grass of the close extends a ring of fine old houses, chiefly Georgian, though some are of earlier date, very severe in their extreme elegance, as if they would say, here is a sanctum designed not for the common herd, but for the elect.

Round Salisbury the country is varied. A mile or two to the north lies the Roman camp of Old Sarum, and beyond are the great, bare stretches of Salisbury Plain. To the west, along the course of the quiet flowing river Nadder, is a thickly wooded valley. It is a pleasant walk from Salisbury, almost entirely under shady avenues, through the little village of Quidhampton to Wilton. Wilton House, standing in beautiful grounds, is one of the most interesting mansions in the neighbourhood. It was built from the designs of Holbein and Inigo Jones, and it was here that Sir Philip Sidney wrote his *Arcadia*. One could not have imagined more appropriate surroundings for such a task. The house contains one of the most important collections of paintings by Vandyck in the country.

South of Salisbury, following the course of the Avon, we find still another type of country, a country of undulating Downs, full of many delightful villages—Downton, Redlynch, and many others.

There are two types of buildings which are typical of the district. In the barer regions the use of stone is common, and some of these cottages in general style bear some resemblance to the stone houses of the Cotswolds, though they cannot approach them in elegance. The thatched roof of the Wiltshire cottage is distinctive, and gives a much homelier appearance.

There is another style of building which under different names extends west to Dorsetshire and Devonshire, and is probably a survival of an older style of building than the timbered cottage. In it the walls are built merely of mud hardened in the sun. In more important buildings, of course, such a soft and crumbling material has to be strengthened by stone or brick-work, but in the little cottages of the Wiltshire valleys walls of mud alone are sufficient for the homely cottages. The simplicity of the thatched roof is repeated in the uniform wall surface below, and nothing could be quieter or less pretentious than such a building nestling under the shade of the luxuriant trees. They seem almost like beehives, so primitive do they appear.

On inquiry I found the system of building was as follows :—

The foundations are generally of stone or of brick, and are carried about a foot above the ground-level. Sometimes at the corners one finds an oaken post, or some brick-work, but not as a rule in the smaller buildings.

The clay, which is a local product and contains a large proportion of gravel and small stones, is dug out and mixed with water. A little straw is added to bind it, and the mixture trodden well together, or sometimes beaten with a wooden beater. A course of some eighteen inches or even two feet wide, and about eighteen inches in height, is then laid down, and the sides cut square with the trowel. This is allowed to stand for a day or two till it is hard, and then another layer is added, and so on till the wall is complete. In the finished work the joining of the different layers is plainly visible.

Sometimes the mud surface is left just as it is, but often, as a protection from the weather, it is plastered and covered with a coat of yellow wash. A typical example of these little mud cottages may be seen in the plate opposite page 98.[1]

I examined a stable built in this fashion. Where the corners had been broken away it was repaired with brick ; otherwise it was entirely a mud dwelling. And so soft is the material that the horse moving restlessly in its stall, and rub, rubbing against the wall, had gradually worn it away to a depth of eight or nine inches. It would be an easy matter to cut one-self out of such a prison.

1. Plate 21 in this edition

PLATE 33. THE CLOTHES-BASKET

PLATE 34. NEAR HEATHFIELD, SUSSEX

PLATE 35. AT WEST TARRING, NEAR WORTHING

PLATE 36. AT TOLLER, DORSET

PLATE 37. AT PAIGNTON, SOUTH DEVON

PLATE 38. BY A DEVONSHIRE COTTAGE

PLATE 39. AT WHITTINGTON, GLOS.

PLATE 40. AT A COTTAGE GATE, DORSET

The ordinary walls by the roadside are often built of this same material, and here we have a characteristic feature of the Wiltshire roads. In all cases where a mud wall is used, though the sides may be left as they are, a protection of some kind is absolutely necessary for the top, or the rain would soon crumble the wall away. And so these roadside walls have a little roof of thatch, projecting about nine inches on each side, which throws off the rain. Not only is the effect very picturesque, but the little roof forms quite a welcome shelter in a shower. Sometimes, instead of thatch, tiles are used, and I have seen corrugated iron put to the same use.

In Dorsetshire much the same character of building prevails. Round Bridport, once the seat of a thriving hemp industry, stone buildings are common, but they possess little in the way of distinctive features of their own.

In Somerset we have some fine types among the larger houses, and it would be difficult to imagine a more beautiful specimen of the English homestead than the farmhouse in the plate facing page 190.[1] It seems to have grown in its surroundings and to be part of them, so well does it harmonise with the landscape.

But in Devonshire one gets a fashion of building

1. Plate 45 in this edition

highly characteristic of the district, and differing considerably from other styles. The buildings are of mud, or cob, as it is called here, but instead of being merely little cottages, they are often of considerable size.

The system is much the same as in Wiltshire, but in larger buildings it is evident that a somewhat more elaborate treatment is required. Sometimes a foundation of brick or stone is built; sometimes the walls are built direct on the rock, which is levelled for the purpose. Masonry is used round doors and windows, and where required, support is given to the walls by great stone buttresses. These are generally placed at the ends of the buildings, but sometimes occur at intervals along the front. They are usually built of a slaty stone, and are not plastered, but merely covered with a coat of whitewash.

The chimneys of the Devonshire houses are very distinctive, as may be seen from the examples in the plates facing this page and page 164.[1] They are great square things, unornamented save for a course of bricks round the top, almost like small factory chimneys. Sometimes the chimney is plastered all over and yellow washed like the rest of the building.

There could not be a greater contrast than that

1. Plates 37 and 38 in this edition

between the stone buildings of the Cotswolds and the cob buildings of Devonshire. The first are elegant to the point of severity, the second are picturesque to the point of untidiness. But still the Devonshire cottage has a charm of its own of which the native never tires, and which, on a closer acquaintance, gradually becomes evident to the stranger.

'Here at least,' writes Mr. G. Ll. Morris, 'is the spirit of the old builders that gave much and asked little—that gave us the buttressed, plastered, and whitewashed cob walls, the big square chimneys, and the somewhat casually thatched roofs of the Devonshire and Somersetshire cottages. There is not one built severely square, and but few have a complete gable or hip. They follow the contours of the ground, haphazard—picturesque and rambling, like the talk of a native, they are as pleasant to look at as the other is to listen to. The walls never seem upright, the windows appear to be placed anywhere, and the thatch does not cover the roof so carefully and neatly as it might do. Casual and careless, with many faults and no finish, might fairly be the description given them by a foreigner. Every part seems wanting, but the whole has that indefinable charm that probably springs from their relationship to the surroundings. Of these cottages it can be truly said, that they are growths of the soil, trimmed and clipped somewhat by man, but never enough that they can be described as " works of art." There is a little design perhaps, some putting together of mud material, some thatch, and that is the cottage! The rest somehow escapes us, for one finds the trees, the hedgerows, the orchards, the sun, the rain, and the rocks have a real and intimate part in the result.'

CHAPTER IX

THE STONE HOUSES OF THE COTSWOLDS

'But I would be where Windrush sweet
Laves Burford's lovely hill;
The old grey town on the lonely down
Is where I would be still.'

HENRY CHARLES BEECHING.

HITHERTO we have confined ourselves to the wood-lands and plains of the southern counties, where the typical farms are the half-timbered house, and the still more humble mud-walled cottage. In these districts stone is only used, even when plentiful, for churches, noblemen's seats, and such other important buildings. The fact is, that the expense of working stone outweighed other considerations, even where its first cost was not great. The mason was not so common a figure in those days as he is now, and he might have to be fetched from a distance, while for the ordinary post and panel house, the village car-penter was architect and builder both, and was always on the spot.

In the northern and barer parts of the country, the moors of Yorkshire and the mountains of Wales, the country was too poor to maintain other dwellings than the rugged castles of the nobles and the rude hovels of the peasantry ; but in the Cotswold district we had quite another set of conditions.

Here we have a rolling upland district spreading over several counties, where a great belt of limestone strikes across the country, forming a plateau of from eight hundred to twelve hundred feet high. Almost treeless, except in the valleys, yet this was a rich country, and not a poor one. For those Cotswold slopes, bare and uncultivated, were the richest pasture-lands in England, and the wool-growing industry, which we have seen exercised so evil an effect on the prosperity of the agricultural districts, here had its headquarters. The fleeces of the Cotswold sheep were famous for their weight and fine quality, and were eagerly sought after, both at home and abroad.

When the price of wool rose, landowners in other parts hastened to put their lands under pasture, but the wool they produced could never equal that of the Cotswold hills, which, with their short crisp turf, formed an ideal grazing ground. It was the over-production of these inferior grades of wool that ultimately lowered the prices, but even when it ceased to be profitable elsewhere, the wool of the Cotswold district always found a ready market.

From the end of the fourteenth to the beginning of the seventeenth centuries was the period during which the neighbourhood reached the height of its prosperity, and it was then that the beautiful grey towns were built, with their fine churches, elegant houses, and wide, pleasant streets.

The wool merchants of Campden, Burford, and the other little Cotswold towns were among the wealthy men of England, and when they came to build their houses, with a fine instinct they used the material that lay ready to their hand, the limestone hidden under the turf of the softly moulded hills. But not only did the prosperous merchants fill the little towns with beautiful buildings, so that the High Street of Campden has hardly its equal in England, but in the country districts the farmhouses and humble cottages were built of the same materials, and in the same style. This style was absolutely different from that of the half-timbered structures a few miles away in the Warwickshire valleys, for the hard limestone demanded quite a different treatment, but is full of the same sensitive feeling for proportion, the same simplicity and directness, and the same air of homely comfort.

It is a beautiful country, and though the railways cross it in several places, yet the bulk of it lies off the beaten track, and is little frequented by the tourist. There is something big and inspiring about the wide sweeps of unbroken pasture-land, the shoulder of the hill right up against the white clouds and the blue sky beyond. The woodlands have their charm, their sense of mystery, but these windy uplands seem to have something of the boundless freedom of the sea. It is a place to go to breathe, to get one's lungs expanded.

The life of the shepherd has a strange fascination. It is older than agriculture; in it we seem to join hands with the patriarchal days. The advance of science has done much to upset the whole system of the old-fashioned farmer, with its patent manures, steam-ploughs, and reaping-machines, but science does not seem to have much to say regarding so old an occupation as this. In essentials it is what it was in the dawning of history. Lambs continue to be born in just the same way, and to require just the same care. The March storms are just as destructive as they were three hundred years, or a thousand years ago, and as much beyond human control. The shepherd now perhaps does not look the picturesque figure he once did, but at heart he is much the same. He is a lonely man, with the far-away look in his eyes that men have who see few of their kind, and is glad to talk when he descends for a little into the more populous lowlands.

It was in the Cotswold country, and from the life, that Shakespeare studied the shepherds and shepherdesses that in his pages are so different from the ordinary lay figures of the pastoral poet. You can see the country in his descriptions, ' Those high wild hills and rough uneven ways draw out our miles and make them wearisome,' and the talk of his shepherds has the very smack of the hillsides. It was a fortunate thing for English literature that Shakespeare spent his youth in the countryside, and knew all the phases of its outdoor life as few poets have known it before or since. And it is characteristic that, after a busy and successful life in the city, the larger and more peaceful life of the country draws him back again to spend there the evening of his days.

Since then others have known the fascination of the Cotswolds, and other poets have sung of their beauties. It is a district for the antiquary to linger in. William Morris dwelt on its outskirts, where they reach down to the upper Thames, and loved its old towns. In the words of Mr. W. H. Hutton: 'There are many who could say in all candour, "Doubtless, God might have made a better country, but certainly He never did." Everywhere the sheep crop the close fields, or clamber over the rough roads, or wend their way in long droves up the lanes. Everywhere the roses hang in thick clusters from the houses, or circle in rich profusion on the laden bushes. Everywhere the old grey walls surround and complete and tone the picture. Even the country graveyards, half neglected as they are, are here of a different sort to those we wanderers know. The barrel-shaped summits to the tombs, the cherubs of a quaint, unusual type, the cypress and yews, immemorial like some of those towers and arches which stand out among them, all are solemn, dignified, even a little pompous. Gently, peacefully all the village goes to rest in this untended garden, and we come to covet such a rest as this, and such a grey headstone with such quaint heralds of immortality.'

It would be difficult to find a stone more suitable for building purposes than the Cotswold limestone. It lies only a few feet below the surface, and is soft and easily worked when newly quarried, but becomes hard by exposure—an excellent weathering stone. In colour yellowish at first, it bleaches after a time, and then takes on all sorts of soft, rich hues, every variety of beautiful grey, especially when lighted up by sunshine. Such a material had more than a local reputation. Not only is the stately town of Bath built of this stone, but near Burford is the quarry which supplied the stone for St. Paul's Cathedral. A strange contrast that the stone from the one quarry should blacken in London smoke in one of the greatest buildings in the land, while that from another but a short distance away has formed little cottages that nestle in the neighbouring valley. Christopher Kempster was the master-mason who superintended the work at St. Paul's, and the quarries are still called by his name, ' Kit's Quarries.'

Every village once had its local quarry, but most of these are now disused, for when a new house is built now, no one thinks of using the home materials. It is cheaper to use imported bricks.

The chief difference that strikes one between the Cotswold houses and the half-timbered cottages of the plains, is that the former seem much more formal and precise. They are built in a more unyielding material. The oak timbers in the frames of the latter have a certain elasticity. They twist and bend like the timbers of a ship. In thatched roofs also there is a softness and fulness of outline, very far removed from the clean-cut, decided lines of the slate roofs of the limestone houses. There is not the happy-go-lucky, go-as-you-please sort of feeling about the stone houses. They seemed to have stayed as they were built, while the others have changed and altered with the times. Thrown out a wing here, added a lean-to there, until the original plan is half effaced. But in the eighteenth century the prosperity of the district died down, and since then there has been little cause to add to the stone houses, which to begin with were planned on a generous scale.

Perhaps there is just a tinge of bleakness about them. Though much more elegant, they do not look so cosy as the half-timbered cottages. They have a colder air, as if they belonged to a severer and more northern clime, and remind one a good deal of the best class of old stone buildings in the lowlands of Scotland.

The plan is usually a parallelogram as in other old cottages. The house is just one room in depth, of a breadth of from sixteen to eighteen feet, and this the roof crosses in one span. If more accommodation is wanted, wings are added, the plan being L-shaped, E-shaped, or H-shaped, but in all cases the single span roof is retained. Where the cottage is small the roof has usually no lateral support, but just rests on the walls, which are often pushed outwards by the strain.

But this system of building one room deep only had its disadvantages. It left none of the little nooks and crannies which are so convenient. There were no store cupboards, no larders, nothing but the four bare walls. Often there were no corridors or passages, and one room opened into another. Frequently you had a series of bedrooms built in this way, all opening one out of the other.

In a large farmhouse of the old style the master and mistress had their room in the centre at the top of the staircase. All the other bedrooms were only accessible through it. To the right was a door opening to rooms occupied by the sons of the house; through these were the quarters of the male servants. To the left was another door leading to the apartments of the daughters and the maid-servants. When the family retired, therefore, the head of the house had the whole household under lock and key. Nowadays, however, we find generally that a separate staircase has been added to the servants' quarters.

The bedrooms in these houses had often another disadvantage. In the seventeenth century, when many of them were built, it was thought for some reason to be unhealthy to have the sun shining into a bedroom, and so they were built to face the north and east, and are apt to be chilly and cold.

In fact, despite their exquisite proportions and fine air of elegance, one can find many faults in these old houses. Their admirable simplicity was obtained by ignoring many things which to modern ideas are absolutely necessary. In the words of an enthusiastic admirer, 'the breadth of wall space was unbroken by the vertical lines of down pipes, which cut all modern buildings into strips, and such things as ventilation pipes and sanitary monstrosities were unknown.' In other words, there was practically no provision for sanitation, and all water had to be carried from the well in buckets. Also the houses are often built on a slope, and the lower rooms are so damp that most of them are now disused. The stone floors, indeed, were laid direct on the ground, damp courses were unknown, so no wonder that the houses were not dry. Many of them, too, had no foundations whatever, and in some cases the turf was not even removed, the walls being begun simply on the ground. Eaves, gutters, or downspouts are unknown, for lead is only used for glazing ; the rain runs off the roofs on to the ground and soaks in at the base of the walls, which thus gets decayed and worn. The site was frequently very ill-chosen, often lying low and close to streams, while no attention was paid to aspect. It is just as well to remember these things, for we are apt to laud the old buildings as everything that is good, while we condemn the modern as everything that is bad, whereas it is just as indisputable that we have improved in matters of comfort and sanitation as that we have sadly deteriorated in matters of artistic excellence.

The walls, as a rule, are from eighteen inches to two feet thick. Sometimes the stone is used just as it comes from the quarry, sometimes it is roughly dressed. In any case the window openings are finished with dressed stone, as is also the doorway, as may be seen in the plate facing page 168, which is a typical example of the Cotswold cottage. At times the walls are very badly built, being a mere shell filled with rubble ; on other occasions the building is excellent. Often the surrounding walls and even the outbuildings are

1. Plate 39 in this edition

built without any mortar, like the Scotch dry-stone dykes, but so well is this done, that it is impossible to dislodge the smallest stone.

On examining the illustration we notice several features which differ from those of the ordinary type of cottage. First are the two little gables, magnified dormer windows, running straight up from the walls. These are very common in the district, and make a much larger and lighter upper room than the low-set windows under the eaves. Very noticeable, too, is the line of stone moulding or drip-stone round the tops of the windows, acting the double part of turning off the rain, and affording a pleasing piece of decoration. The graceful chimneys in this case rise from the centre of the ridge-tree, with very charming effect. Sometimes the chimneys are at the gable ends, and often the kitchen chimney is a separate stack built on outside the house. In that case we have a very large fireplace, often six feet or more in width, and from four to five feet high, crossed by a stone arch or a great oak beam. Wood was the usual fuel, and pots and kettles were not placed on the fire, but hung from an iron trivet hinged to the wall.

Often an ingle-nook was formed on each side of the fire, a seat being hollowed out of the thickness of the wall just large enough for one person, and arched above his head. On each side a few inches up were hollows for the elbows or for a glass as the case might be. In village inns these corners, in spite of the pungent smoke from the fire, are reserved for prime favourites, or old customers. Sometimes the ingle-nook is lit by a little window. The flue is tall and tapering, and goes straight up, being open to the sky. As a rule, it smokes badly.

The partitions between the rooms are generally not of stone but of oak frames filled in with lath and plaster, or with oak-panelling. The staircases are usually circular and of stone, built with a central newel like the stair in a church-tower.

The roofs are covered with stone slates not unlike the Horsham slabs, but much smaller in size. The roof, it will be seen from the plate, is quite high in pitch, unlike the Surrey and Sussex roofs, where the heavy Horsham slabs necessitate a flatter roof. The slates are laid with great care, the thickest being placed at the eaves and the thinnest at the top, and are fastened down with oaken pegs.

They are obtained from the local quarries, and are not split by hand, but in a very curious manner. During the season (May till October) they are quarried and laid out on the ground in thick slabs. There they are allowed to remain all winter. They absorb a certain amount of moisture which works in between the layers of the stone. Then come the winter frosts, and the water freezes and expands. The result is that in the spring a few taps with the hammer suffices to divide the thick slab into a series of thin flakes. If, however, the winter is mild, the stones do not split, and there is nothing for it but to allow them to lie for another year. It is a leisurely way of working that sounds very attractive.

These grey slates covered with lichen are very beautiful, and are almost imperishable. Roofs three hundred years old are as good as new. If the wood foundation is decayed, or the pegs have given way, the slates can be taken off and rehung. Like the old tiles, the old slates are much better than the modern ones. The mechanical precision with which the latter are turned out, all as smooth and thin as possible, and the edges exactly true, makes them have a hard and cold effect. There is no variety in a roof of such slates, but the old varied in size and thickness. Also the old oak-laths on which the original slates were hung were often not quite straight, and the result was a beautiful wavy line.

The old slates too were more durable. Being rough, they did not lie absolutely close (perhaps, however, they leaked on this account), and thus the wet dried out of them easily, for there was free ventilation. The new fit so closely, that there is no circulation of air, and when moisture thus collects, there is more chance of the frost getting in and doing damage.

A very quaint and interesting feature in those cottages is the series of little name-plates on the walls, little chiselled tablets of stone giving the name or initials of the owner, and usually the date. It is the owner's name evidently, not the builder's, for in some cases there are several such inscriptions on the same cottage. In the plate already referred to, a sundial is placed just between the two windows. Simple though these name-tablets are, they are executed with skill and freedom, and form a pleasant ornament.

Although there are no other stone cottages of the elegance of those of the Cotswold country, yet stone cottages are not uncommon in other districts. In the plate facing page 178,[1] a Wiltshire cottage, we have several features of a similar character. The grey stone, the central chimney, the drip-stone— all these are not unlike the Cotswold type. The roof of thatch, however, gives quite a different character

1. Plate 42 in this edition

to the house, and makes it look shaggy and unkempt, a great contrast to the clean lines of the Cotswold slates. The chimney, too, is of brick, and of a different shape from the slender Cotswold shafts, and brick is used again in the side wall.

CHAPTER X

OLD FARMHOUSES

' Here the architect
Did not with curious skill a pile erect
Of carved marble touch or porphyry,
But built a house for hospitality.'

CAREW.

IN the days when England was an agricultural country, and this was from the beginning of our civilisation until the eighteenth century, the farm was the centre round which the national life revolved. The classes above and below were both dependent on the farmer.

The lord of the manor, great man though he was, drew the main part of his income from the rent of his farms. The rest he obtained from the rents of humbler dwellings, whose inhabitants were chiefly dependent on the farmer for employment. For the landowner was not a great employer of labour. There were the house-servants, of course, and perhaps a forester or two, gamekeepers, and gardeners, but these formed a small proportion of the population of the countryside. It was the farmer who was the great employer of labour. He was the peg on which the whole social system depended. Pull him out and it collapsed.

Any one could draw the rents and play the grand gentleman. Any able-bodied man could fill the rôle of the farm-labourer. But the farmer was the trained man, whose special knowledge was required to direct operations ; who knew how things should be done, and saw that they were done.

In these days of scientific training and agricultural colleges we are apt to scoff at the old farmer, but though he had not the opportunities his descendants have, yet he had as thorough a knowledge of his work as was possible in those days. And it takes more to make a farmer than most folks think.

He had to know, in the first place, all the different varieties of soil in his district. Their properties, and how to utilise these ; what crops they would bear, and so on ; and how to manure them, and bring the best out of each. Often in one narrow farm the soil would vary in almost every field, from rich loam or heavy clay to the merest gravel and sand.

Then, too, he had to know all about the various crops. He had to be able to take up a sample of grain in his hand, and gauge in a moment its qualities and its market value.

He was a breeder of horses, cattle, sheep, pigs, and poultry. He had to know all about those animals, their points, their values, and, most important of all, their diseases, for the vet. could not be called in at every moment.

He had to manage a small army of workmen, too, and to organise his work so as to be ready to take the fullest advantage of, and to suffer least from, the vagaries of a most capricious climate.

And in addition to all these personal qualities, he had to be a man of some means, for farming then, as always, meant capital.

And so take him all round, the old British yeoman, the real old John Bull, represented what was best in his country—a man solid and prosperous, full of common-sense and of the knowledge which is based not on book-learning, but on experience.

Each farm, with its attendant cottages, formed a little community complete in itself ; an establishment fitted with all the requisites for carrying on the great agricultural industry. Every one was dominated by this, and thought, spoke, and lived in terms of agriculture. Spring was the time of sowing ;

summer, of growth; autumn, a reaping-time; winter, the dead lull, when the earth sleeps to refresh herself for another year of reproductive activity. Men watched the skies anxiously in those days, not idly as we do now, and it was little wonder that they talked about the weather. Rain or the lack of rain were serious matters; a sudden storm might bring ruin in its train, and a bad season was little less than a national calamity. The little villages were composed of farm-labourers, with the blacksmith, the carpenter, and a few small tradesfolk, all ultimately dependent on the farms for their livelihood. Even the market-towns, where one finds a fully developed civic life, and where manufactures have sprung up and trade abounds, owe their existence to the fact that they are the depots to which the farmer brought his produce for sale. Each farmer from all the country round came once a week to this common centre. Thus the wealth of the country was brought together for distribution, and thus the farmers were able to ex-change produce, and carry on all the business of their complicated calling.

A healthy, open-air life it was, and bred a race of vigorous men. And in the old ways the farmer was, as a rule, a prosperous man.

The life of the farm-labourer, too, though hard, was not without its compensations. There were holidays and fair days, and, the greatest of all these rural festivals, the harvest-home. For then the labour of the year had been brought to a triumphant conclusion ; in spite of wind and weather, the good corn was gathered in and safely stored, and the farmer and his people rejoiced together. The tables groaned with abundance of homely fare, the home-brewed ale flowed freely, and the feasting and dancing were kept up till morning.

And the farmhouse reflects the life of which it is the centre. It is absolutely homely, for its owners were free from the affectations of the upper classes, and built for use and not for show, but comfortable and complete, for there was no lack of money to supply everything that was required. It is this air of purposeful utility which is the great merit of the farmhouse. It is the highest development of the cottage style of architecture, everything good, even luxurious, but simple, and designed for work, not for leisure. Every detail bespeaks the object of its existence. The house in the centre, roomy, snug, and comfortable ; the garden at one side ; then the yard, with its clustering outbuildings, its granaries and barns, cattle-sheds, kennels, and poultry-houses.

They date, those old farmhouses, chiefly from the time of Queen Elizabeth, where, as we have seen, such an epidemic of building spread over the land, and every one who could, pulled down his old house and set up a new one. And among them are numbered many of the finest half-timbered houses which we have. For those farms had a better chance of survival than the smaller cottages. They were larger buildings, and more strongly built, and have been kept in better repair. Their size gave greater scope to the architect, and though the object for which the house is built is never lost sight of, yet it is full of pleasing decorative features. The roof forms are very varied, and the tall, delicately shaped chimneys, so finely grouped, give a distinction which we look for in vain in any modern building.

Sometimes the farmhouse is of a still earlier date, and is, in fact, an old manor, which has come down in the world, but which still holds up its head, dignified and stately, amid surroundings which are sometimes a little incongruous. Such a house we find in the Hall Farm of the Poysers, so beautifully described by George Eliot. The great gate in front has grown rusty, and weeds cluster about it. The front door is almost never opened, and the front rooms seem empty, for the focus of life has shifted round to the back, where, radiating from the kitchen as a centre, all is activity.

Such a farm I knew in Wirral, Bidston Old Hall, a fine stone-built Tudor manor-house. But now it is merely a farmhouse, and you can have tea any afternoon in the great hall, which is much frequented by cyclists for this purpose.

Sometimes in such a farmhouse you will find that the old lofty hall has been cut in two by a floor and the upper part converted into bedrooms.

In the farmhouse the principal room is the kitchen, often a huge room some thirty feet long and nearly as broad. The floor is stone-flagged, and sometimes a well opens direct from the kitchen floor. Formerly the unmarried male labourers lived and boarded at the farm, so the oak table was of a size sufficient to seat about a dozen people. On one side of it a bench was fixed to the wall, on the other was a movable bench. The fireplace was capacious, with a cosy ingle-nook. There used to be fine old iron fire-dogs, and often a beautiful cast-iron fire-back, but now these are seldom to be seen. Very beautiful and elaborate, too, were the wrought-iron cranes, the work of the village blacksmith, from which were suspended the great pots and kettles.

From within one sees the object of the huge chimney which projects from the side of the house like a buttress on a church. The upper part is used as a bacon-loft. Rows of iron ribs extend across it, each with a number of hooks from which the sides of bacon are hung, and round the sides are other hooks for the smaller pieces, chops and bones, etc. Oak or ash wood was used for curing the bacon, all pine and such resinous woods being avoided.

Then close to the kitchen is the dairy, cool and sweet and fresh, and it is cheering to know that this branch at least of the farming industry continues to prosper. Sometimes in the dairy windows you will find beautiful old ventilators of pierced lead.

Often the farmhouse was furnished with a capacious cellar, not only for the home-brewed beer, but also in cider counties for cider.

Nowadays there is not very much left of the fine old furniture which used to fill the farmhouses. Unfortunately the taste of the inmates turns more to flashy and pretentious modern stuff, and it is seldom one finds one of the old kitchens unspoilt and filled with the old simple furniture.

Oak was the original material for all the furniture in those houses, and when later the use of mahogany became general, the old forms were repeated in this wood, but rather lighter in style as befitted the harder and heavier material.

Next in importance to the oak trestle-table, which I have already mentioned, were the great oak dressers, garnished with dishes which stood up against the wall. Sometimes in these each successive shelf as you went upwards projected more, giving an overhanging effect like that of the old houses in town streets where space was valuable.

Then there were huge linen chests or hutches, often richly carved, and light tables were used in the parlour. Sometimes these were gate-legged, either circular or elliptic in shape; now and again one came across such a curious shape as a triangular three-legged table.

Chairs were once made of oak, heavy and square and solid, but these cumbrous forms gave place to the lighter wheel-back and Windsor chairs, the seats of which are formed of a solid piece of elm, or the rush-bottomed chairs with sparred backs.

In village inns one may still find the high-backed oaken settle, so useful to screen one from the draught of the door, and I have seen it too in a little Cheshire cottage, but it is comparatively rare.

In the bedrooms now and again we find great oak beds, the head and foot boards moulded and panelled, while beautiful old chests of drawers, both in oak and mahogany, are not uncommon.

A very curious structure is seldom seen, but was once used extensively. I refer to the bed-warmer. This was a frame-work or crate of oaken hoops, two or three feet long by about two feet broad, and about a foot deep. On the bottom in the centre was fixed a plate of iron, and a trivet stood on this in which was inserted a brazier of hot coals. Another plate of metal in the top of the frame prevented the bedclothes being scorched, and the machine must certainly have answered its purpose effectively. But the copper or brass warming-pan superseded the older wagon.

Once the kitchen-dresser must have been bright with pewter, but there is little of that left now, though one now and again still comes across a pair of fine brass candlesticks. The old crockery, too, was much more decorative than what is now in use, but crockery, alas, has not a long life, and what few old examples remain are quickly picked up by the dealers.

A curious implement which one often comes across

is the rushlight-holder, for in the days before gas
and mineral oils, the poorer folks could not afford
candles, and rushlights were their substitutes until
well on in the nineteenth century. The rushes were
peeled all but a narrow strip of the green rind, which
was left to hold the pith together, and were soaked
in melted fat. They must have required a lot of
attention as they burnt at the rate of an inch every
two minutes, and as only about an inch and a half
projected from the holder, the light would thus need
to be mended every three minutes.

Outside the house we come to still closer terms
with the old outdoor life. The yard is a perfect
artist's paradise. The irregular masses of outbuildings,
some with thatched roofs, some tiled, the sides of most
covered with weather-boarding of a deep blue-black
tint, shading into purples in some lights like a crow's
feather, afford a fine contrast to the house. Over
by the duck pond is a rough thatched shelter standing
quite open, and supported on stout posts only, under
which stand carts and agricultural implements. Such
a shed looks strange to one coming from the north.
On the north side of the Border such an open shed
would not stand a winter; the first gale would send
the roof flying into the next field.

Very beautiful are some of the old barns, huge buildings that would contain £1000 worth of wheat when they are full, but that is seldom the case now, for it does not pay to grow wheat on English farms. Formerly the corn used to be threshed (and threshed by means of the old hand-flail, not by the steam-thresher), as soon as possible after harvest, and then the straw being sweet and fresh was eaten readily by the cattle in the yard. Allowed to stand for a month or two in the stack, it becomes stale and musty, and the animals won't touch it. The old barns were beautiful structures inside, the framing of timbers being all displayed to the eye, and the roof as elaborate as the old wooden roof of a church. The floors are of oak or of stone, preferably the former, as stone is apt to bruise the grain.

Now and again one comes across a fine old granary of even greater size than the barns, such a one as that illustrated by Miss Gertrude Jekyll in her *Old West Surrey*. This is a great rectangular structure, built on a solid brick wall as foundation, and the floor thus standing some eight feet above ground-level. The open part underneath is used as a shelter for carts, etc. The upper part is supported on solid piers, and has a flight of steps leading up to it on one

PLATE 41. COTTAGE GATE, SPRING

PLATE 42. AT WISHFORD, WILTS.

PLATE 43. HELL FARM, SIMONSBURY, DORSET

PLATE 44. WYLDES FARM, NORTH END, HAMPSTEAD HEATH

PLATE 45. THE DAIRY FARM, NEAR CREWKERNE, SOMERSET

PLATE 46. AT BURTON BRADSTOCK, DORSET

PLATE 47. FROM SANDHILLS COMMON, WITLEY, SURREY

PLATE 48. THE OLD MALT-HOUSE, BROOK, SURREY

side. The roof is tiled, and the walls, too, are covered with weather-tiling. In the door is a little hole for the cat !

Round the farmyard sometimes runs a hedge, sometimes an old post and rail fence, to divide it from the fields.

Formerly many English farmers, the descendants of the old yeomen, owned their farms, and in 1688 figures were published giving the number of these landowning farmers as 180,000. But few of these remain. They dwindled away during the nineteenth century and now agriculture is more or less stagnant. In the neighbourhood of the large towns dairy-farming is indeed always profitable, and fruit-growing is carried on with more and more success; but English wheat now cannot compete with the supplies poured in from abroad, and the stackyard of the farmer stands empty. The labourers, too, that filled the cottages and lived on the farms are finding more profitable work in the towns, and year by year the country becomes more desolate.

More capital, too, is required to farm now success-fully, so the lot of the farmer to-day is hardly an enviable one.

Almost as important as the farmer was the miller,

and usually the mill is a much older building than the farm. A solid building of stone it often was, and belonged to the lord of the manor, who thus exacted a toll from all the farmers in the district. Sometimes the mill belonged to the monks of the abbey, and but seldom was the actual property of the miller. Both wind and water-mills were in use from an early period, and indeed water-power was turned to many other accounts than driving a mill for the grinding of corn. In the sixteenth century we hear of a great hammer being used in the Sussex ironworks, driven by a water-wheel, and we may suppose that this is only one among many similar uses.

Something between the farmhouses and the manor-houses in style are the old vicarages and parsonages which one finds in the more rural districts. More elegant than the farms perhaps in style, but less in size, they are often beautifully complete, and their small grounds laid out with elegance and taste, for they have always been in the hands of men with a certain amount of leisure, and with refined and elegant tastes.

During the eighteenth century many beautiful buildings were added to the little county towns, and though these were seldom or never of the cottage class, we frequently find a farmhouse or rectory among them. And often the country lawyer or doctor's house is of this elegant style. To me the simple square house comes as a welcome change after the more irregular and rambling buildings; and to modern tastes, in many ways, the high-ceilinged, well-proportioned rooms, with their chaste mouldings, are preferable to the low ceilings and great beams of the half-timber houses, however picturesque these may be.

CHAPTER XI

OLD COUNTRY INNS

'I'll lead you now to an honest ale-house, where we shall find a cleanly room, lavender in the windows, and twenty ballads stuck about the walls.'   IZAAK WALTON.

THINGS were very different in England at the time when the old country inns were built. Imagine the railway system, which spreads its filaments from end to end of the country like a great spider's web, swept away entirely. Imagine all telegraphic communication stopped, so that news must travel slowly by road. Imagine a condition of things, when horse-traction was the speediest method of travel, and poor men set out with a bundle on their backs to tramp hundreds of miles on foot.

In these days of speedy travel and evening papers, when the news of all the world is known all over the world simultaneously, we find it difficult even to realise such a condition of things. We have almost

lost the conception of the road as a great thoroughfare
between one part of the country and another. We
seldom think of it as more than a means of communication between house and house, village and village
' It is no distance,' we say; ' you can go by road.'
But in the days when the old inns flourished, the
white ribbon of the king's highway, winding up hill
and down dale, diving into woods, crossing bridges,
and losing itself for a while in busy towns, was the
only thoroughfare. It was the link between village
and village, town and town, county and county, and
this since the very beginning of our civilisation.

Some of our main roads are still the old roads first
made by the Romans ; one or two, notably the famous
track along the Downs from Winchester to Canterbury,
are older still. And during all those centuries, until
little more than sixty years ago, they were the arteries
through which circulated, except where it went by
water, all the traffic and travel of the country. The
carriages of the nobility, the post-horses or the chaise
of the private traveller, the stage-coach, men on
horseback, men on foot, tinkers, pedlars and packmen, drovers, wagoners for the heavier traffic,—
all these passed to and fro along the highway.
Shelter at night and refreshment by the way was,

of course, necessary for all those wayfarers, so the inn is an institution as old as the road itself.

In the Middle Ages it was supplemented to some extent by the monastic houses, but these, as a rule, entertained only two classes, the very rich and the very poor. The first were received by the monks because they dare not refuse them, but many were their complaints regarding the excesses of their unwelcome guests. The monastery door, however, was always open to the poor man, who was never turned empty away.

The inns were used by the people between these two extremes, for they were too miserable for the nobility, too expensive for the poor. They were frequented by the smaller gentry, merchants, packmen, and other traders. The entertainment was poor enough; a number of beds were spread out in one room on the floor, and each guest bought what food he required. The prices charged were notoriously high, so much so that Edward III. passed a law against 'the great and outrageous cost of victuals kept up in all the realm by innkeepers, and other retailers of victuals, to the great detriment of the people travelling across the realm.'

Still, to judge from Chaucer's picture of the Host of the Tabard Inn, the innkeeper might yet be a good fellow, and give his customers more in good fellowship than ever was paid for in their reckoning.

In the Louterall Psalter is a most interesting drawing of an English inn of the fourteenth century. It is a half-timbered house of some size, for it has not only two stories, but a gable wing. The roof is thatched, and at both wing gable and end gable is an ornamental barge-board. Out of the window, which is evidently unglazed, projects a long pole with a large bunch of twigs at the end—the bush, which was the common sign of the inn, and is referred to in the proverb, ' Good wine needs no bush.'

In addition to these inns were ale-houses by the wayside, where refreshment could be had, but not accommodation for the night. Chaucer's Pardoner, when asked to contribute his tale, stops at one of these houses.

> ' But first,' quod he, ' heere at this ale stake
> I wol bothe drynke and eten of a cake.'

In the sixteenth century, the poet Skelton writes of just such a wayside tavern, situated near Leatherhead in Surrey, where the ale-wife—' Her nose som-

dale hooked, and camously croked '—is noted for the
quality of her brew.

> ' She breweth nappy ale
> And maketh thereof port sale
> To travellers, to tynkers,
> To sweters, to swynkers
> And all good ale drinkers.'

But such houses then, as now, did not always
enjoy a good reputation, and the poet remarks on the
different manner in which it was approached by its
various customers.

> ' Some go streyght thyder,
> Be it slaty or slyder ;
> They holde the hye waye,
> They care not what men say,
> Be that as be may.
> Some loth to be espyde
> Start in at the backe syde,
> Over the hedge and pale
> And all for the good ale.'

In the reign of Henry VIII. coined money was rare
and in bad repute, and so we hear that

> ' Instede of coyne and monny
> Some brynge her a conny,
> And some a pot with honny,
> Some a salt, and some a spone,
> Some theyr hose, some theyr shone.'

By that date, however, inns of a better class had

arisen ; indeed some of the fine old examples still existing to-day, such as the Crown Inn at Chiddingfold, the Star Inn at Alfriston, and the Mermaid at Rye, are of quite as early a period as this. During Elizabeth's reign the inns became still more commodious and comfortable. Harrison tells us that 'those townes that we call thoroughfares have great and sumptuous inns builded in them.' And the humble bush no longer served as a sufficient indication to the passer-by, for he remarks on 'the gorgeousness of their verie signs at their doores, wherein some doo consume thirty or forty pounds—a meere vanitie in mine opinion, but so vaine they will needs be.' Unfortunately few, if any, of those old signs still exist.

A good picture of the best class of inn in the early seventeenth century is given by Fynes Moryson, an English gentleman just returned in 1617 from making the grand tour, wherein he contrasts the English inn with its continental rivals.

'I have heard some Germans complaine of the English Innes by the high way, as well for dearnesse, as for that they had onely roasted meates. But these Germans landing at Gravesend, perhaps were injured by those knaves, that flocke thither onely to deceive strangers, and use Englishmen no better, and after went from thence to London, and were there entertained by some ordinary Hosts of strangers, returning home little acquainted with English customs. But if these strangers had knowne the English tongue, or had had an honest guide in their journies, and had knowne to live at Rome after the Roman fashion (which they seldome doe, using rather Dutch Innes and companions), surely they should have found that the World affoords not such Innes as England hath, either for good and cheape entertainment after the Guests own pleasure, or for humble attendance on passengers, yea, even in very poore villages, where if Curculio of Plautus should see the thatched houses, he would fall into a fainting of his spirits, but if he should smell the variety of meates, his starveling look would be much cheared. For assoone as a passenger comes to an Inne, the servants run to him, and one takes his Horse and walks him till he be cold, then rubs him, and gives him meate, yet I must say that they are not much to be trusted in this last point, without the eye of the Master or his Servant to oversee them. Another servant gives the passenger his private chamber and kindles his fier, the third puls of his bootes, and makes them cleane. Then the Host or Hostesse visits him, and if he will eate with the

Host or at a common table with others, his meale will
cost him sixpence, or in some places but fourpence
(yet this course is lesse honourable, and not used by
Gentlemen) : but if he will eate in his chamber, he
commands what meate he will according to his appetite,
and as much as be thinkes fit for him and his company, yea, the kitchen is open to him, to command
the meat to be dressed as he best likes ; and when
he sits at table, the host or hostesse will accompany
him, or if they have many Guests, will at least
visit him, taking it for curtesie to be bid sit downe ;
while he eates, if he have company especially, he shall
be offered musicke, which he may freely take or refuse,
and if he be solitary, the Musitians will give him the
good-day with musicke in the morning. It is the
custome and no way disgraceful to set up part of
supper for his breakfast. In the evening or in the
morning after the breakfast (for the common sort
use not to dine, but ride from breakfast to supper time,
yet comming early to the Inne for better resting of
their horses) he shall have a reckoning in writing,
and if it seeme unreasonable, the host will satisfy
him, either for the due price, or by abating part,
especially if the servant deceive him any way, which
one of experience will soon find. . . . One that eates

alone in his owne chamber with one or two servants
attending him, perhaps upon reckoning may spend
some five or six shillings for supper and breakfast.
. . . I will now only add that a Gentleman and his man
shall spend as much, as if he were accompanied with
another Gentleman and his man, and if Gentlemen
will in such sort joyne together to eate at one Table,
the expences will be much diminished. . . . One
horse's meate will come to twelve pence, or eighteen
pence the night, for Hay Oates and Straw, and in
Summer time commonly they put the horses to grasse,
after the rate of three pence each horse, though some
who ride long journies will either keepe them in the
Stable at hard meate as they doe in Winter, or else
give them a little oates in the morning when they are
brought up from grasse. . . . Lastly, a Man cannot
more freely command at home in his owne House,
then hee may doe in his Inne, and at parting,
if he give some few pence to the chamberlin and
ostler, they wish him a happy journey.'

The next stage in the history of the country inns
is the coming of the stage-coach. We are apt to look
back on the old coaching days with contempt, as
primitive in the extreme, but that is far from being
the case, for the mail-coach system was brought to a

state of great perfection. Stage-coaches existed during the eighteenth century, but they were in the hands of private companies, and were local concerns, generally more or less mismanaged, so that the service between even the largest towns was sluggish and irregular.

The establishment of the Government mail-coach system was due to the energy and enterprise of John Palmer, a native of Bath, and proprietor of the Theatre Royal there. Having great difficulty, owing to the wretched means of communication between Bath and London, in arranging for a punctual succession of good actors at his theatre, he turned his attention to the question of the improvement of locomotion. The result was a comprehensive scheme for establishing Government coaches on all the great roads, carrying the mails and a limited number of passengers, at the rate of ten miles an hour.

The scheme met with opposition everywhere, but when submitted to Pitt, the great statesman recognised its feasibility, and on 8th August 1784 the first Government mail-coach started from London at eight in the morning, reaching Bristol at eleven the same night. The system was a complete success, and Palmer, its originator, became Surveyor and Comptroller-General of the Post Office, M.P. for Bath, and a wealthy and important man.

De Quincey, in his English Mail-coach essays, vividly describes the starting of the Government mails from the General Post Office in London, and shows to what perfection by that time—the beginning of the nineteenth century—the system had been brought.

' From 8 P.M. to fifteen or twenty minutes later, imagine the mails assembled on parade in Lombard Street, where at that time . . . was seated the General Post Office. In what exact strength we mustered I do not remember ; but, from the length of each separate *attelage*, we filled the street, though a long one, and though we were drawn up in double file. On any night the spectacle was beautiful. The absolute perfection of all the appointments about the carriages and the harness, their strength, their brilliant cleanliness, their beautiful simplicity—but more than all, the royal magnificence of the horses—were what might first have fixed the attention. Every carriage on every morning in the year was taken down to an official inspector for examination ; wheels, axles, linchpins, pole, glasses, lamps, were all critically probed and tested. Every part of every carriage had been cleaned, every horse had been groomed, with as much vigour as if they belonged to a private gentleman. . . . The guards, as being officially his Majesty's servants, and of the coachmen such as are within the privilege of the Post Office, wear the royal liveries, of course, and as it is summer . . . they wear on this fine evening these liveries exposed to view. without any covering of upper coats. . . . Every moment are shouted aloud by the Post Office servants, and summoned to draw up, the great ancestral names of cities known to history through a thousand years—Lincoln, Winchester, Portsmouth, Gloucester, Oxford, Bristol, Manchester, York, Newcastle, Edinburgh, Glasgow, Perth, Stirling, Aberdeen—expressing the grandeur of the empire by the antiquity of its towns, and the grandeur of the mail establishment by the diffusive radiation of its separate missions. Every moment you hear the thunder of lids locked down upon the mail-bags. That sound to each individual mail is the signal for drawing off ; which process is the finest part of the entire spectacle. Then come the horses into play. Horses ! Can there be horses that bound off with the action and gestures of leopards ? What stir !—what sea-like ferment !—what a thundering of wheels !—what a trampling of hoofs !—what a sounding of trumpets !—what farewell cheers ! '

In De Quincey's opinion the modern mode of travelling by rail cannot compare with the old mail-coach in grandeur and in power. The speed of the train, he says scornfully, may be there, but you have no direct consciousness of it. You only know you have been travelling at the rate of forty miles an hour, because you left London at such and such an hour and are now in York. With the mail-coach, however, all the time you felt the speed with which you were travelling. ' The vital experience of the glad animal sensibilities made doubts impossible on the question of our speed ; we heard our speed, we saw it, we felt it as a thrilling ; and this speed was not the product of blind, insensate agencies, that had no sympathy to give, but was incarnated in the fiery eyeballs of the noblest among brutes, in his dilated nostril, spasmodic muscles, and thunder-beating hoofs. . . . But now, on the new system of travelling, iron tubes and boilers have disconnected man's heart from the ministers of his locomotion. Nile nor Trafalgar has power to raise an extra bubble in a steam-kettle. . . . Tidings fit to convulse all nations must henceforwards travel by culinary process, and the trumpet that once announced from afar the laurelled mail, heart shaking when heard screaming on the wind and proclaiming itself through darkness to every village or solitary house on its route, has now given way for ever to the pot-wallopings of the boiler. Thus have perished multiform openings for public expressions of interest, scenical yet natural, in great national tidings —for revelations of faces and groups that could not offer themselves amongst the fluctuating mobs of a railway station. The gatherings of gazers round a laurelled mail had one centre, and acknowledged one sole interest. But the crowds attending at a railway station have as little unity as running water, and own as many centres as there are separate carriages in the train.'

All of which is very eloquent pleading for an absolutely untenable case. But it must be admitted that there is some truth in the charges brought against the modern system as regards its lack of dramatic and scenical effects. The railway runs on a track of its own, not along the public highway; the train does not pull up with a flourish at the inn in the main street, but glides into a hidden station. The telegraph, too, is secret and noiseless, and though the newspaper boy, with his shrieks of ''orrible murder,' may sometimes achieve the sensational, he falls short of the dramatic.

The centre of all the noise and bustle was the inn.

It was railway station, posting establishment, news depot, hotel, all in one. The mails were dropped there, the coach changed horses there, the travellers alighted there to sleep, or for refreshment. It maintained a perfect army of ostlers, and stable-boys, and hangers-on, and to these the greatest man on earth was the driver of the royal mail. Here is his portrait sketched by Washington Irving :

‘ Wherever an English stage-coachman is seen, he cannot be mistaken for one of any other craft or mystery.

‘ He has commonly a broad, full face, curiously mottled with red, as if the blood had been forced by hard feeding into every vessel of the skin ; he is swelled into jolly dimensions by frequent potations of malt liquors, and his bulk is still further increased by a multiplicity of coats, in which he is buried like a cauliflower, the upper one reaching to his heels. He wears a broad-brimmed, low-crowned hat ; a huge roll of coloured handkerchief about his neck, knowingly knotted and tucked in at the bosom ; and has in summer-time a large bouquet of flowers in his button-hole, the present, most probably, of some enamoured country lass. His waistcoat is commonly of some bright colour, striped, and his small-clothes extend far below his knees, to meet a pair of jockey-boots which reach about half-way up his legs.

' All this costume is maintained with much precision ; he has a pride in having his clothes of excellent materials ; and notwithstanding the seeming grossness of his appearance, there is still discernible that neatness and propriety of person which is almost inherent in an Englishman.

' He enjoys great consequence and consideration along the road ; has frequent conferences with the village housewives, who look upon him as a man of great trust and dependence ; he seems to have a good understanding with every bright-eyed country lass. The moment he arrives where the horses are to be changed, he throws down the reins with something of an air, and abandons the cattle to the care of the ostler ; his duty being merely to drive from one stage to another. When off the box, his hands are thrust into the pockets of his greatcoat, and he rolls about the inn yard with an air of the most absolute lordliness.'

Life seems to go on in a more leisurely way in such places, and we have time to ' take our ease ' at such an inn.

All over the country, in the fishing inns of the

Scotch Highlands, in the Welsh valleys, where the inns are full of old furniture and carved oak chests, in Lancashire and in Cheshire, in Surrey and in Kent, one meets the same kindly welcome. And the smaller and more primitive the inn the better.

I remember once spending a few days in the tiny inn of a little Kentish village. It was a fine old building. Etchings by Dendy Sadler adorned the walls of the parlour, for it was a favourite haunt of that artist, and above the kitchen fireplace was a portrait of the innkeeper by the same hand. When I arrived, I was asked whether I would dine alone or with the family, and promptly chose the latter course as much more interesting. One was treated with a pleasant mixture of familiarity and deference. When one of the men came in from work, and was about to sit down to dinner in his shirt-sleeves, he was hustled out of the room to reappear in a black coat, and with his face polished and shining. In the evening the villagers dropped in, and one saw a little bit of the old country life.

The yard of the inn was a commodious place, and when the coach arrived, presented a scene of great activity. Round it were ranged the stables for the horses, the coach-house, and a huge shed for the accommodation of the lumbering wagons, each with its huge canopy bulking almost as large as an ordinary cottage. For the coaches were the greyhounds of the road; they travelled light, and carried little luggage beyond the mails and the passengers' personal luggage. The great bulk of the traffic went by wagon, which not only had greater carrying capacity, but carried goods much more safely than the coach. The wagon, too, was the only conveyance at the disposal of those who were too poor to afford the coach. And so the wagoner was a well-known figure on the country roads.

' It is a cold and stormy night, and I'm wet to the skin ;
   I'll bear it with contentment till I get to the inn ;
   And then I'll sit a-drinking with the landlord and his kin.
      Sing Wo! my lads; sing Wo!
      Drive on, my lads, heigh-ho!
   Who would not live the life of a jolly wagoner?'

Who would? we should be inclined to say in these degenerate days.

But with the coming of the railways the picturesque mail-coaches disappeared, and the wagon traffic dwindled and died away except in the remoter districts. By the middle of the nineteenth century desolation had spread over the country roads. For the first time in their history they ceased to be the only thoroughfares, and in many cases they became

quiet backwaters, where the carriages of the local
gentry, and the carts of the farmer and the village
tradesmen, supplied all the wheeled traffic, while
tramps and vagrants, and perhaps a pedlar or two,
were the only pedestrians. The inns fell upon evil
days ; from busy houses of call frequented by travellers
of all degrees, they dwindled, except in the larger
towns, to the position of mere village public-houses.
And so, despite the improved means of transit between
towns, the country waxed lonelier and lonelier.

Tom Hughes, in *Tom Brown's Schooldays*, bemoans
the fact that the youth of the day (about 1857) spend
their vacations flying over the Continent, and do not
know their own country.

' All I say is, you don't know your own lanes, and
woods, and fields. And as for country legends, the
stories of the old gable-ended farmhouses, the place
where the last skirmish was fought in the civil wars,
where the parish butts stood, where the last high-
wayman turned to bay, where the last ghost was
laid by the heels, they 're gone out of date altogether.

' Now in my time, when we got home by the old
coach, which put us down at the cross-roads with our
boxes, there we were fixtures till black Monday came
round. We had to cut out our own amusements

within a walk or ride of home. And so we got to know all the country-folk, and their ways, and songs, and stories by heart, and went over the fields, and woods, and hills again and again, till we made friends of them all.'

Curiously enough, since then the pendulum has swung back again, and the old roads are once more busy, the old inns once more humming with life. The coming of the bicycle was the beginning of the change. The Cyclists' Touring Club was formed, every one cycled, and the British public rediscovered the country. When cycling ceased to be the amusement of the upper classes, the workers took it up, and now on every holiday swarms of cyclists pour out of the large cities and spread themselves over the map of England.

The latest phase is the coming of the motor-car. Now the wealthy man can travel by road as speedily almost as by train, and with more comfort. We hear outcries about the dangerous state of the roads owing to motor traffic, but we had almost forgotten what the roads were for, and had taken them to be mere tracks for foot-travellers. In the old coaching days, the village street could never have been a safe playground for children, for the stage-coach was much less under control than the modern motor-car.

And so prosperity has come back to the old inns. The old yard has become a garage, and petrol is supplied instead of oats and hay. Travellers do not stay the night, as a rule, for distances have shrunk, and the motorist, except in case of mishap, is not often benighted on the road. The inn has become more an eating-house, and as this it plies a busy trade, for a motor carries nearly as many passengers as the old coach, and for one coach that passed, we have now a hundred motor-cars.

In the future we may look for a much greater development of this road travelling, the railways being used more for goods traffic only, so that the old inns have doubtless many years of prosperity still before them.

If one were asked the chief characteristic of these country inns, the feature which distinguishes them from the hotels of the towns and cities, one would say it is a certain air of homeliness and heartiness which clings to them. Your host is really your host, and does his best to make you comfortable. He does not merely serve you with the precision and accuracy of an automaton, but imparts to his ministrations an air of hospitality. There is a more human feeling in the air which harmonises with the old-world aspect of the house.

CHAPTER XII

OLD GARDENS

'What more delightsome than an infinite varietie of sweet-smelling flowers ? decking with sundrye colours the green mantel of the earth, the universal mother of us all, so by them bespotted, so dyed, that all the world cannot sample them, and wherein it is more fit to admire the Dyer than imitate his workmanship. Colouring not only the earth, but decking the ayre and sweetening every breath and spirit.'

WM. LAWSON.

THE origin of the garden is lost in the mists of antiquity. Wherever man reared himself stately dwellings he seems to have surrounded them with fair gardens. For in the early days, when nature was wild and uncultivated, and the fields of the husband-men were but patches in the midst of the untamed wilderness, man shrank from nature, and within the precincts of his own dwelling wished to drive away all suggestion of her vastness and insecurity. And the garden presented nature shorn of all her terrors.

Nowadays the face of the land is so trimmed and softened by the hand of man that we tire of smiling fields and orchards, and long for something wild and free. We call this getting back to nature, but such a feeling is really the product of a very high degree of civilisation, and shows how far we have travelled from the old primitive conditions. The love of nature, as we feel it, was much too sophisticated an emotion for the natural man. He was so close to nature, he was dependent on her every whim. How could he take an æsthetic pleasure in watching her moods when he had so great reason to fear their results. The storm which we watch with such keen enjoyment might in a few moments render him penniless and homeless. The waves at which we smile from the deck of a great liner would in a moment overwhelm the frail fisherman's cobble. The primitive man deified the forces of nature. It is only modern man who has ceased to fear them.

The evolution of man, in fact, is the history of his never-ceasing struggle with nature. At first, natural forces dominated him entirely. Now, though still dependent to a large extent on nature, he has bit by bit wrested the power from her hands, put a harness on her neck, and made her do his bidding.

Still, she is a changeable and capricious servant, and when she rises in her wrath even modern man stands baffled and humbled. There is no answer to the question, ' Hast thou entered into the springs of the sea? or hast thou walked in the search of the depth? Who hath divided a watercourse for the overflowing of waters; or a way for the lightning of thunder?' 'Out of the south cometh the whirlwind, and cold out of the north,' and man is powerless to interfere.

But the old attitude is changed with increasing knowledge and power. The unknown is no longer filled with superstitious terrors, the modern man loves it as a field still unexplored and unconquered.

Even Shakespeare, whose outlook in many ways is so modern, has not our feeling for nature. Even where he sees its grandeur, as in the storm scene in *King Lear*, it is not with exultation, but feeling to the full all its terrors. It is only in her milder aspects that nature seems to charm him. ' Under the greenwood tree,' he sings, ' Here shall he see no enemy, but winter and rough weather.' Or 'when daffodils begin to peer.' The nature he loved was like an extended garden or park. The physical aspects of wild nature were too present for it to be enjoyed by our fathers. Ways were rough and 'roads were foul.' There were no railways, no macadamised roads, no waterproofs, no umbrellas. It is an open question if we should enjoy the wildness of nature if we were shorn of all our little comforts and snug shelters.

So our forefathers loved to surround themselves with a garden, a fence between them and the outer world. Here they stole from nature her sweetest charms, but admitted nothing harsh or rude. The fairest plants, the most fragrant flowers, the richest fruits, widespreading shady trees; these were surrounded with a high wall, to shut out any wild intruders.

When we seek for human origins we turn our eyes to the East, and Eastern lore is full of beautiful gardens. The Bible tells how God planted a garden in Eden, and later that He walked there in the cool of the day. Everywhere in those parched lands the cool shade of the garden is the refuge from the heat and glare of the day.

Omar Khayyám sings continually of the garden, the rose, and the nightingale, and the *Arabian Nights* are full of gardens of delight.

But where the Eastern garden was a green shelter from the blaze of the sun, the air musical with the tinkle of falling water, our northern gardens were built more as shelters from the bleak winds, facing south to receive all the sunshine that might be, and store it up in masses of brilliant flowers.

The oriental garden may be seen in Spain, for the

Moor brought it there, a patio or courtyard, surrounded by white walls, where the sunshine is tempered by awnings, and a fountain plays in the centre, while wreathing vines overhead make a cool shade. But within its circling walls the English garden laid bare its green bosom to the sun, till the terraced slopes basked in the warm rays, drinking in the golden sunshine with the same avidity as the gardens of the parched lands sucked up the moisture.

When the garden first came to England, who can say ? Certainly in the Middle Ages it was the accompaniment of the lady's bower in every noble-man's residence, and the monasteries enshrined rich orchards within their grey walls.

Chaucer gives us a sweet picture of a garden in the Franklin's tale :

> ' May hadde peynted with his softé showres
> This garden full of levés and of floures,
> And craft of mannés hand so curiously
> Arrayéd had this gardyn, trewély,
> That never was ther gardyn of swich prys
> But if it were the verray Paradys.
> The odour of flourés and the freshé sighte
> Woldé han makéd any herté lighte
> That ever was born, but if to greet siknesse,
> Or to greet sorwé, helde it in distresse ;
> So full it was of beautie with plesaunce.'

And James I. of Scotland, during his captivity in
Windsor Castle, first saw his lady love, who afterwards
became his queen, walking in the garden below his
prison window :

'A garden faire, and in the corners set, an arbour green.'

The classic gardens of Italy are famous, and we
may still see their pale splendour in two charming
paintings by Velasquez of the Villa Medici, where
he stayed for some weeks during his visit to Italy.
These formed the models for the rest of Europe in
Renaissance times, when Italy was the fountain-head
of culture and of art.

When Henry VIII. began to rear his huge palaces
of Nonsuch and Hampton Court, the garden became
part of a grand architectural scheme, and this fashion
was followed in Elizabethan times, when the noblemen
were building mansions which almost vied with the
royal palaces in splendour. In all parts of the country
these beautiful formal gardens were laid out, until
in the eighteenth century the debased craze for
landscape-gardening arose.

The old style where the garden was part of the
architectural plan, and acted as a sort of link
between the rigidity of the building and the freedom
of nature, was founded on reason and good taste ;

the other was merely a neglecting of all rules of order and proportion, and only succeeded in giving a parody of nature. In the times of Walpole many beautiful old gardens perished to make way for atrocities in the new 'picturesque' style, and now they are few and far between. Still they linger, and here and there you may find even to-day a fine old house set in its appropriate garden, like a picture in its frame.

But happily the garden was not confined to the houses of the wealthier classes. John Worlidge, writing in 1677, says of it that 'such is its pre-excellency that there is scarce a cottage in most of the southernmost parts of England but hath its proportionate garden, so great a delight do most men take in it.'

It was in Elizabethan and Jacobean times that the popular interest in gardening arose, and even Puritanism, which suppressed so much that was joyous, could scarce forbid such an innocent recreation.

In 1618 there was published in London a most delightful little book on gardening, 'being the labours of forty-eight years of William Lawson,' as sweet and fresh as a nosegay of flowers. It breathes the spirit of the true lover of nature, and especially the lover of flowers. Gardens, says the author, were made for delight.

'For it is not to be doubted but as God hath given man things profitable, so hath hee allowed him honest comfort, delight, and recreation in all the works of his hands. Nay, all his labours under the Sunne without this are troubles and vexation of mind: For what is greedy gaine without delight, but moyling and turmoyling in slavery? But comfortable delight, with content, is the good of everything, and the pattern of heaven. . . . And who can deny but the principall end of an Orchard is the honest delight of one wearied with the works of his lawful calling? The very workes of and in an Orchard and Garden are better than the ease and rest of and from other labours. When God hath made man after his owne Image, in a perfect state, and would have him to represent himselfe in authority, tranquillity, and pleasure, upon the earth, he placed him in Paradise. What was Paradise but a Garden and Orchard of trees and hearbs, full of pleasure? and nothing there but delights.'

In the sweetness and freshness of his diction Lawson reminds us of Izaak Walton, and he has much of the sunny temper of the immortal angler. A lovable

PLATE 49. WITLEY POST OFFICE

PLATE 50. A WILTSHIRE COTTAGE

PLATE 51. IN A SURREY GARDEN

PLATE 52. A DORSET GARDEN

PLATE 53. HOLLYHOCKS

PLATE 54. WATERING FLOWERS

PLATE 55. BLUEBELLS

PLATE 56. AT GRANNY'S

man we feel at once, and with fine instincts and perceptions. There is a touch of Gilbert White in this passage on the birds :

' One chiefe grace that adornes an Orchard I cannot let slip ; a brood of nightingales, who with severall notes and tunes, with a stronge delightsome voyce, out of a weake body, will beare you company night and day. She loves (and lives in) lots of woods in her hart. She will helpe you to cleanse your trees of caterpillars, and all noysome wormes and flyes. The gentle Robin red-breast will helpe her, and in winter in the coldest stormes will keepe a part. Neither will the silly wren be behind in Summer, with her distinct whistle (like a sweet Recorder) to cheere your spirits.

' The Blackbird and Throstle (for I take it the Thrush sings not, but devours) sing loudly in a May morning, and delight the eare much (and you need not want their company if you have ripe cherries or Berries), and would as gladly as the rest doe your pleasure : But I had rather want their company than my fruit. What shall I say ?   A thousand of pleasant delights are attended in an Orchard ; and sooner shall I bee weary than I can reckon the least part of that pleasure which one that hath and loves an Orchard may finde therein.'

One is glad to note his sturdy common-sense; the throstle's song is very sweet, but when it comes to sacrificing his fruit for it, he draws the line there. The whole book is full of practical wisdom. The first sixteen chapters are strictly devoted to the business of gardening. It is only in the seventeenth and last, where he discourses on 'ornaments,' that he gives his fancy play.

His opening words in chapter i. ought to be wrought in letters of gold above every garden door.

'The Gardner had not need be an idle or lazie lubber, for so your Orchard . . . will not prosper. There will ever be something to doe. Weeds are alwaies growing.'

One would have loved to meet this old gardener, to have sat under his trees and eaten his fruit, and listened to the nightingale sing with a 'stronge delightsome voyce.' The saying that he must be a good man who loves animals must be still more true of the lover of plants and flowers.

In Yorkshire his home was (one wonders how he heard the nightingale so far north), and it calls up a vivid picture of the old-fashioned garden to read only the list of his flowers. 'The rose red, damaske, velvet, and double double province rose, the sweet

muske rose double and single, the double and single
white rose, the faire and sweet-scenting woodbine
double and single ; Purple cowslips, and double cowslips, and double double cowslips ; Primrose double
and single, the violet nothing behind the best .for
smelling sweetly. A thousand more will provoke
your contente, and all these by the skill of your Gardner
so comely and orderly placed in your borders and
squares, and so intermingled, that none looking
thereon cannot but wonder, to see what Nature
corrected by Art can doe.'

Thank Heaven we can still find those old-fashioned
plants now and again in an unpretentious little
cottage garden, and there they seem to be just in their
proper setting.

In village rectories, too, we sometimes find on a larger
scale one of the real old-style gardens. For the tide
of renovation that swept away so much that was old
and beautiful in the large houses often passed by
the rectory and the farm, so that we have there pre-
served many things which in the manor-house and
the nobleman's seat have been lost. One can
wander between narrow walls and deep lanes of
clipped yews, and find the quaint knots, as the old
flower-beds were called, all ablaze with sweet-smelling

flowers. Time seems to have stood still in such old gardens, and the grey sundial to have made but a pleasant jest of recording the passing hours.

There seems to be no yesterday and no to-morrow in places like these. The lichen must always have been there on the grey stone, the red tiles green with moss. The old gardener, with his ruddy face like a ripe pippin, and bent frame like twisted apple-boughs, could never have been young except in heart, and there he will never grow old. The very butterflies that flutter idly in the sunshine cannot be the things of an hour that they are elsewhere. Such is the magic spell that haunts this green quietness.

But when we reach the cottage garden we come to the dearest and most familiar garden of all. It is too modest to have any formal plan save of the simplest nature, just as the cottage itself is what necessity and convenience has made it, but it retains more of the old charm than you will readily find elsewhere. For the village folks are the most conservative of all classes in the community. They it is who have been least touched by the industrial changes which have made the modern commercial world. After all, in spite of patent self-binding machines and steam-threshers, the alternation of seed-time and harvest is just the same as ever it was. It is the same good brown earth that brings forth its fatness ; they plough the same fields that their grandfathers ploughed before them. The same landscape meets their eyes, the same river flows down by the mill. The mill is some four hundred years old, the little grey church is nearly as old again, while the cottages themselves have seen close on three centuries. A few modern agricultural implements make little difference amidst such antique surroundings ; they disturb its peace a little like a passing motor-car, and then quietness settles down again.

And so it is with a special pride that the cottager clings to his garden. Away back in the past his forefathers owned in a sort of way their own little strips of the common land, and now this is all that is left to him. Still, such as it is, it is his own, and his labour there is truly a labour of love. If you look through all the illustrations of this book you will not find one cottage, no matter how humble, that has not its little garden decked with flowers. And it is such a sweet margin to a home, this little area of fragrance, that it makes any other surroundings seem formal and even mean.

In its small space it contains so much. Flowers in profusion everywhere. Roses tended with loving

care, for the rose is the cottager's flower *par excellence*.
Tall holly-hocks reaching almost to the thatched
eaves, sweet-smelling wallflowers spreading their
fragrance far out into the dusty road. Pansies—
heart's-ease is the homelier name—and in their season,
snowdrops, crocuses, primrose and violet. The more
material part is not neglected, for away behind you
will find a goodly store of vegetables. A row or two
of peas and beans, turnips, carrots, lettuce, cabbage
and cauliflower, and a patch of rhubarb, with its great
spreading leaves, in the corner by the hedge. It
reminds you of old William Harrison's garden, of which
he was so proud. ' For mine owne parte,' he says, ' let
me boast a little of my garden, which is but small, and
the whole area thereof little above three hundred
feet of ground, and yet such hath beene my good
lucke in purchase of the varietie of simples, that
notwithstanding my small abilitie there are verie neare
three hundred of one sort and other conteined therein,
no one of them being common or usuallie to bee had.'

You do not look for rareties in the cottager's garden,
just the sweet, homely flowers, and the wholesome
vegetables. Fruit-trees, too, are there, fine old apple-
trees, pears, plums, and thick-set little bushes, with
currants red and black and gooseberries galore. Some-

times there is a little bit of glass, a cucumber frame
or two, where the valued pot plants are brought on
till they can be displayed in the window.

By the hedge next the field you will find now and
then, standing on a thick little wooden bench, a hive or
two of bees, thatched with straw, and looking like a
miniature cottage; a busy and populous little home, with
its winged denizens flying busily to and fro. William
Lawson, like many a modern writer, had a great belief
in the profitable nature of bee-keeping. ' Store of bees,'
he says, ' in a dry and warme bee-house comely made
of fir-boards, to sing and sit and feede upon your
flowers and sprouts, make a pleasant noise and sight.'
One likes the way the word ' sing ' is used here ; it is
such a happy tribute to this unconscious, cheerful
music. He goes on : ' For cleanly and innocent Bees,
of all other things, love and become and thrive in an
Orchard. If they thrive (as they must needs if your
Gardiner be skilful and love them, for they love their
friends, and hate none but their enemies), they will,
besides the pleasure, yield great profit to pay him
his wages. Yea the increase of twenty Stockes or
Stooles, with other fees, will keepe your Orchard.

' You need not doubt their stings, for they hurt not
whom they know, and they know their keeper and

acquaintance. If you like not to come amongst them, you need not doubt them, for but neere their store, and in their own defence, they will not fight, and in that case onely (and who can blame them?) they are manly, and fight desperately.'

The old gentleman evidently knew his bees, and entered into their little lives with insight and sympathy.

Perhaps once the cottage garden was modelled on formal lines (in the plate facing page 270[1] we see the remains of some clipped yews), just as the cottage itself was based on a regular plan. But as the one has been added to continuously, an offshoot here, a lean-to there, so the garden has adapted itself to the requirements, and now perhaps its greatest charm is its informality and lack of arrangement. The flowers cluster together in a companionable sort of way. There is no room to be stiff in the little enclosure, and so they are all on familiar terms.

The flower-garden in front and the kitchen-garden behind, that is the usual plan, and from the road the cottage seems embedded in a nosegay, while the presiding spirit, an old woman in a white cap, stands at the door. I remember years ago finding such a little cottage in Kent. Its soft red brick was half hidden

1. Plate 61 in this edition

with trailing wisteria, one mass of pale-purple blossoms. I stopped to sketch it, and the dear old lady came out and refreshed me with cowslip wine and little home-made cakes.

One of the characteristic features of these cottage gardens, especially the front part, is the style of their fences or other boundaries. The commonest, and perhaps the most beautiful, is the simple green hedge, but this is not always a sufficient protection, as it is apt to grow open at the foot. Sometimes wooden fences are used, and these are of various sorts. In Berkshire, and also in Wiltshire, you may still see wattled fences, in the Cotswolds dry-stone walls, and in Devonshire stone walls covered with white-wash, while in Cheshire stone slabs placed on end are sometimes used, as in the north of Scotland.

The gate itself is often an ornamental feature. Fine wrought-iron examples of simple design are still to be met with in out-of-the-way places, but for the most part they are of wood. Sometimes a rose or other bush will be trained into an arch above the gate, and in Scotland two rowan-trees are often so inter-twined, for no witch or fairy can enter through the arch of rowan.

I once spent some months in a little Cheshire

cottage. The cottager was of an old country stock, and had been trained as a gardener, but had been dragged into the great industrial machine, and now worked among the engines in a neighbouring factory. But he did not care to stay in the model village provided for the hands, where the gardens were laid out in a uniform fashion, and a man paid to keep them so, while the very children were forbidden to play about the doors, lest they should make the place untidy. No, he preferred to walk a mile or so to his work, and to live in a little cottage of his own (at a higher rent), where he could work in his garden of an evening.

There was great excitement when the time of the village flower-show came round, for it is a great event in the rural year. For nearly a week before, a pet currant bush had been covered with a cloth to keep back the clusters of fruit that were ripening just a little too quickly. And woe betide the hapless wife or daughter who dared to pluck the said berries for culinary purposes. I am glad to think that they won the prize.

There is this feature about a small garden: it is your own. It is a just arrangement of Providence that, when a man increases his possessions beyond a very narrow limit, they pass out of his hands, and he virtually ceases to own them. The nobleman's garden is his in name. But in reality it belongs much more to the head-gardener. Within its gates the latter is a veritable despot. He dispenses 'his fruit' and 'his flowers' to the household, often with a most niggardly hand. He cannot bear to denude his greenhouses to decorate a paltry drawing-room.

Robert Louis Stevenson, in his delightful portrait of the old Scotch gardener, tells how, 'if you asked him to send in one of your own artichokes, "That I wull, mem," he would say, "with pleasure, for it is mair blessed to give than to receive,"' and I know many other people who groan under the tyranny of their gardeners.

But the man who cultivates his own little patch, who takes 'al the paines,' as William Lawson says, the rough work as well as the smooth, owns it in a real sense.

He takes an actual pride in the growth of his plants; they have grown up so entirely under his hand, that he forgets the silent part of nature, and feels as if he himself was their creator. He can enter into the feelings of the old Scotchman just referred to, who, if you remarked how well a plant was looking, 'would gravely touch his hat and thank you with solemn unction, all credit in the matter falling to him. If, on the other hand, you called his attention to some backgoing vegetable, he would quote Scripture: " Paul may plant, and Apollos may water," all blame being left to Providence on the score of deficient rains or untimely frosts.'

For man's greatest delight in this world is to fill, if even to the most limited extent, the rôle of creator. And compared with the making of mere implements and machines, inept and dead, however intricate and curious they may be, what a wonderful craft is this which takes part in the making of living organisms. And your works do not remain so long that they grow stale and wearisome. They live their brief day and then pass away, giving place to a never-ending succession of fresh forms, each as new and fascinating as the last.

CHAPTER XIII

THE OLD VILLAGE LIFE

'Of all situations for a constant residence, that which appears to me most delightful is a little village far in the country: a small neighbourhood, not of fine mansions finely peopled, but of cottages and cottage-like houses, "messuages or tenements" as a friend of mine calls such ignoble and nondescript buildings, with inhabitants whose faces are as familiar to us as the flowers in our garden; a little world of our own, close packed and insulated, like ants in an anthill, or bees in a hive, or sheep in a fold, or nuns in a convent, or sailors in a ship; where we know every one, are known to every one, interested in every one, and authorised to hope that every one feels an interest in us.'

MISS MITFORD.

WHAT, it may be asked, is the secret charm of the old village life, what is it that gives its completeness, a beauty rounded and finished like that of a work of art ?

To enable us to answer the question I cannot think of a better way than to ask what it is that gives the old village homes their characteristic charm. And in answering this, we shall find that the reasons are much the same in both cases.

As we have seen, the outstanding virtue of the old

cottage is its simplicity and its directness. It fulfils the purpose for which it was intended, without any pretensions to be other than it is. Its materials are local materials, it is stamped with the character of its natural surroundings. There is in it an entire absence of the Academic. It relies not on codes of rules, but on tradition—on the old local methods of overcoming the local difficulties. And so it is self-sufficient, self-reliant, and sincere.

And so with village life. It is full of a beautiful broad simplicity and directness. It deals more with essentials than refinements. One finds the genuinely human there, with less disguise than in the cities, where men conceal their individualities under a mask of uniformity. In the village, people are frankly natural. This simplicity is far removed from the ignoble, for its sincerity gives it dignity. The world is so small there, that every one has his distinct place in it, and the result is not a narrowing one on the individual. Rather he is impressed with a serious sense of his responsibilities, of the awful importance of the part he plays. It is when our world is so wide that it dwarfs us to pigmies, that we are apt to become irresponsible and frivolous.

For ages the village worthy has been a butt for

every shaft, but the humour is all good-natured, and the dear fellow is so serious himself, that he cannot be hurt by it. We wouldn't have him different for worlds, and if he had taken himself less seriously, it would have been so much the worse for the interests under his charge. He was the growth of his environment, and fitted it exactly. It is only when viewed from the outside that he becomes comical.

For as Washington Irving points out: ' In rural occupation there is nothing mean or debasing. It leads a man forth among scenes of natural grandeur and beauty ; it leaves him to the workings of his own mind, operated upon by the purest and most elevating of external influences. Such a man may be simple and rough, but he cannot be vulgar.'

Each village was an independent community, and managed its own affairs to an extent of which, in spite of all our apparatus of local government, we have no idea. In the pre-railway days each little colony was more or less isolated, and in winter, when the roads were bad, might be shut off from all intercourse with the outside world for days together. This encouraged a healthy independence and self-reliance. The squire was king in his own village, and ruled it often with a rod of iron. It is no merely fanciful

picture that the poet sketches when he talks of
the

> 'Village Hampden that with dauntless breast
> The little tyrant of his fields withstood';

and the village stocks struck terror into the hearts
of evil-doers.

In such surroundings characters developed in a
natural way, and every old world-village is full of
worthies even to-day. And in times past the types
must have been much more interesting.

First the squire, pictured at his best in Sir Roger
de Coverley, one of nature's gentlemen and the father
of all the countryside. Then comes the rector. He
might be a sweet-tempered old naturalist like Gilbert
White, or he might be learned in divinity. Or, again,
he might be one of your jovial hunting parsons.
'.Difficulties! Doubts! Take a couple of glasses of
port. If that don't dispel them, take two more, and
continue the dose till you have found ease of mind.'
But whatever the line in which his natural tastes
led him, he would have full opportunity to follow it
in his ample leisure. Then the apothecary, 'the official
associate, adviser, comforter, and friend of all ranks and
all ages, of high and low, rich and poor, sick and well,'
the attorney, the farmer, down to the simple cottagers.

There were breaks, too, in the monotony of country
life, harvest-homes, shearing feasts, to say nothing
of country fairs. Even a visit to the nearest market-
town was an exciting event to the good wife, for at
other times she was dependent for her finery on the
visits of the pedlar who displayed his wares on the
doorstep. He was a merry fellow the pedlar, and it
was wonderful the variety his pack contained. ' He
hath ribands of all the colours i' the rainbow ; inkles,
caddises, cambrics, lawns. Why, he sings them over
as if they were gods and goddesses. You would think
a smock were a she-angel he so chants to the sleeve-
hand and the work about the square on 't.' And here
is one of the songs :

> ' Will you buy any tape
> Or lace for your cape,
> My dainty duck, my dear-a ?
> Any silk, any thread,
> Any toys for your head
> Of the new'st and fin'st, fin'st wear-a ?
> Come to the pedlar :
> Money 's a medler,
> That doth alter all men's ware-a ! '

In Elizabethan days, England was a musical country,
but the Puritan spirit, as it rose, endeavoured to kill
this levity. Minstrels were branded as rogues and
vagabonds as early as 1597, and in 1648 the Provost-

marshal was given power to arrest all ballad singers. Organs and lutes were destroyed, and gaiety stamped out with an iron foot. Cromwell's third Parliament ordered the arrest of all minstrels and musicians performing in taverns. But this severity did not entirely succeed, for until recent years music lingered in the villages. Every little church had its band, fiddles and viol, ophicleide and flute. These instrumentalists attended all weddings and other festivals, and at Christmas time trolled out carols in the frosty night air. It is only yesterday since these old village bands died out, and the parish chests still contain their sheets of rudely written music ;—carols, country dances, and old ballads. It is only in Wales that the musical spirit still lingers. There on the summer evenings the youths cluster at the street corner, singing glees and part songs, but elsewhere the villages are mute save for the husky wheeze of a concertina.

It is very curious how little the cottage, and indeed rural life at all, appears in English literature. But in this is revealed a trait of national character. The English are a silent people. The things which matter most are by tacit consent left unsaid. The people who lived in those cottages and loved them are just the people who would never write about them. One might almost say they would never even talk about them, but deep down there was the silent feeling that this was home, the most sacred thing of all to an Englishman.

Before such life could be written about, it had to be viewed from the outside. Sympathetically and with intuition, but still from the outside. Had there been a village Pepys, one might have had the village life from within, but the cottager is a more reticent being, and in his busy, useful life was not addicted to the polite arts of literature. It is a shock to think that in this democratic land a democratic literature is the growth of recent years, but the fact remains. Except in Scotland, the democracy, as a general rule, did not read a generation or two ago. The democratic literature which did exist was not a printed literature. The old ballads sung by the fireside, and at harvest-homes and other merry-makings, were handed down orally from generation to generation, and were much more poetic than modern literature, for one must be a rhymer to catch the ear and hold the memory— who could remember dull stretches of prose ? But when ballads were written down, it heralded the fact that ballad-making was dead. The Robin Hood songs were composed not in the monk's study, but under the greenwood tree, and long after the polite and cultured upper classes had outgrown such childish things, and were students of the classics, the old genuine art of poesy was kept alive in village ale-houses and on village greens. But one gets little of the village life, as a rule, from the old ballads, for, like children's fairy tales, they deal more with legendary and imaginary themes.

And it is not until our own day that this village life is dealt with sympathetically from the outside.

The courtly poets of Elizabethan days found such rustic themes too coarse for their dainty pens unless seen through a rosy haze of idealisation. They give us pastorals instead of country life; instead of yokels we have peasants in Dresden china.

Sir Philip Sidney, the courtier and gentleman *par excellence*, sings not of England, but of Arcadia, of nymphs and shepherds, of Phyllis and Corydon. It is the poetry of a golden age of fancy. Marlowe's shepherd sings to his love and offers her ' silver dishes for her meat,' 'ivory tables,' and other sweet bribes, which do not smack of rural England, charming though they be ; and so on through the list of courtly poets.

Shakespeare alone, with the memories of Warwick-shire lanes and Cotswold slopes in his mind, could not help being natural, true artist as he was. It is

like a breath of fresh country air when he tunes his
rustic pipe. No foppish Corydon pays silken compli-
ments to a pink-and-white Phyllis, but

> ' Dick the shepherd blows his nail
> And Tom bears logs into the hall,
> And milk comes frozen home in pail,
> When blood is nipp'd, and ways be foul,
> Then nightly sings the staring owl ! '

This is the real country life, the same note that
two hundred years later rings in the songs of the
peasant poet Burns.

But it almost seems as if Shakespeare was
ashamed of his rusticity, he allows it so seldom to
appear. It is but by unexpected glimpses that his
knowledge of rural affairs is revealed, and from the
lips of clowns and fools. But he was not a town-bird,
like the most of the other dramatists of his day. The
spell of the country always held him and drew him
back again to spend there the afternoon of his days.
The singer who sang so sweet and natural a song as this :

> ' Under the greenwood tree
> Who loves to lie with me
> And tune his merry note
> Unto the sweet bird's throat,
> Come follow, come follow, come follow.
> There shall he see no enemy
> But winter and rough weather,'

knew the country life, and was familiar with its every charm.

In Milton's *L'Allegro,* we have a hint of rural beauties, but the window with its

> ' Sweet briar or the vine
> Or the twisted eglantine '

is hardly that of the cottage, rather that of the manor, or at least the farmhouse. Still it is a fresh picture of an early morning country scene :

> ' The cock with lively din
> Scatters the rear of darkness thin,
> And to the stack, or the barn door,
> Stoutly struts his dames before.
>
> .   .   .   .   .
>
> While the ploughman near at hand
> Whistles o'er the furrowed land,
> And the milkmaid singeth blithe,
> And the mower whets his scythe,
> And every shepherd tells his tale
> Under the hawthorn in the dale.'

There is mention, too, of the humble dwelling :

> ' Hard by, a cottage chimney smokes,
> From betwixt two aged oaks ' ;

but we must stop here, for Corydon and Thyrsis enter in the next line, and the rural charm has fled.

At a slightly later date this writing of pastorals

has become as artificial as the painting of Watteau, though with much of his dainty charm, and Richard Steele lays down the rules which should govern it.

' An author,' he says, ' that would write pastorals should form in his fancy a rural scene of perfect ease and tranquillity, where innocence, simplicity, and joy abound. It is not enough that he writes about the country; he must give us what is agreeable in that scene, and hide what is wretched. Let the tranquillity of the pastoral life appear full and plain, but hide the meanness of it; represent its simplicity as clear as you please, but cover its misery. As there is no condition exempt from anxiety, I will allow shepherds to be afflicted with such misfortunes as the loss of a favourite lamb, or a faithful mistress. He may if you please pick a thorn out of his foot or vent his grief for losing the prize in dancing, but these being small torments, they recommend that state which only pro-duces such trifling evils.' A charming art, doubt-less, but how remote from the vivid picture of ' Dick the shepherd ' blowing his nail on a bleak hillside.

After these rose-tinted pictures the writings of Crabbe come as a rude blast of realism. The misery

and squalor of rural life is his theme, and he has eyes
for nothing else. Where are your gay shepherds
and shepherdesses ? he asks scornfully :

> 'Peasants now,
> Resign their pipes and plod behind the plough.'

He has bitter gibes for the smug poets who sing so
cheerfully of rural joys :

> 'Or will you praise the homely, healthy fare,
> Plenteous and plain, that happy peasants share?
> Oh trifle not with wants you cannot feel,
> Nor mock the misery of a stinted meal.'

His labourer stalks the earth with the dreary fatalism
of Millet's toilers :

> 'Go then to see them rising with the sun
> Through a long course of daily toil to run ;
> See them beneath the dogstar's raging heat,
> When the knees tremble and the temples beat.
> Behold them, leaning on their scythes, look o'er
> The labour past and toils to come explore ;
> See them alternate suns and showers engage,
> And hoard up ills and anguish for old age.'

And yet, though this is realism, one feels that
it is hardly truth. After all, toil is the common lot
of man, and hard though his lot might be, the rustic
was not overwhelmed with its misery. He had his
joys as well as his sorrows ; the ploughman whistled

to his horses, the milkmaids sang over the milking-pails.

True, in a higher sense, it seems to me, is the picture in Gray's *Elegy*. A life of 'useful toil,' indeed, but relieved by 'homely joys.' 'How jocund did they drive their team afield.' Of course they did; he had seen them do so many a time. And were there not harvest-homes, and Christmas rejoicings, and village fairs, to say nothing of the village love-making in the country lanes? And then the joys of home life. 'The blazing hearth,' the 'busy housewife,' the children running 'to lisp their sire's return.' What better has life to offer than such joys as these? No, one must not dwell too much on the dark side of the picture, though it, too, is a true phase.

Burns in the north country lived this same life of relentless toil, and the struggle was, if anything, harder there than in the south; but he sings of its joys as blithely as any courtly poet in his study, nay, with a smack of honest appreciation which is unmistakably genuine. Amid its bitter trials his big heart can well over with sympathy for the tragedy of even a little field-mouse whose nest he has turned up with the plough.

Goldsmith, also, sings in the happier vein, though

we may suspect that his pictures are not free from idealisation. He gives us, too, an interior, the village inn :

> ' Near yonder thorn, that lifts its head on high,
> Where once the sign-post caught the passing eye,
> Low lies that house where nut-brown draughts inspired,
> Where greybeard mirth and smiling toil retired,
> Where village statesmen talked with looks profound,
> And news much older than their ale went round.
> Imagination fondly stoops to trace
> The parlour splendours of that festive place :
> The whitewashed wall, the nicely sanded floor,
> The varnished clock that clicked behind the door ;
> The chest contrived a double debt to pay,
> A bed by night, a chest of drawers by day ;
> The pictures placed for ornament and use,
> The twelve good rules, the royal game of goose ;
> The hearth, except when winter chilled the day,
> With aspen boughs, and flowers and fennel gay ;
> While broken tea-cups, wisely kept for show,
> Ranged o'er the chimney, glistened in a row.'

The great writers of the early nineteenth century did not work this rural theme to any great extent. The romantic aspects of nature appealed to them more. Byron, Keats, and Shelley—they all wanted wider fields in which to stretch their wings. Wordsworth was a lover of nature, more especially in its mystical aspects; the cottage door presented too obvious an invitation for him.

Sir Walter Scott, indeed, showed the way in his inimitable studies of Scottish rural types, Dandie Dinmont, Edie Ochiltree, the shepherd, the fisherman, the ploughman—these were his characters. Here he struck a vein which has been worked out more fully by his successors, but his scenes are nearly all laid north of the Tweed, among the people he knows best.

It is curious that the beautiful and delicate work of Jane Austen should reflect so little of English rural life. Exquisitely truthful as her delineations are, she moves entirely in the atmosphere of the rectory or the manor-house. She feels that she is getting out of her element when she descends even to a creature of such common clay as a farmer ; her business is with ladies and gentlemen, not with men and women. Her approach to the cottage was seldom any nearer than to make a ladylike sketch of its picturesque exterior, and if she ever does enter its portals, it is when descending like a good angel from her higher regions with comfortable gifts of jellies or of blankets. Mrs. Gaskell, in *Cranford*, gives us more of the charm of the old village life, but she also moves chiefly in the upper circles, and we must turn to the delightful pages of Miss Mitford to find the real village, and really to mingle with the people.

Contemporary with these appears, however, a writer with quite a distinct and original point of view. A man of the new world, not of the old, but withal a man of wide culture and broad sympathies ; a man with a shrewd eye to observe, and a gift of expression which is equalled by few English essayists. For the first time we see the country life of England from the outside, as it strikes the visitor from other lands. And among all Washington Irving's writings, it is his sketches of English rural scenes and rural customs which are most widely read to-day. His *Sketch Book*, with the *Bracebridge Hall* series, has become a classic to which Englishmen now turn to realise the England of an earlier day. What could express the feeling of an English landscape better than the following extract ?

' The great charm, however, of English scenery is the moral feeling that seems to pervade it. It is associated in the mind with ideas of order, of quiet, of sober, well-established principles, of hoary usage, and reverend custom. Everything seems to be the growth of ages of regular and peaceful existence. The old church of remote architecture, with its low, massive portal, its Gothic tower, its windows rich with tracery and painted glass, in scrupulous preservation, its stately monuments of warriors and worthies of the olden time, ancestors of the present lords of the soil ; its tombstones, recording successive generations of sturdy yeomanry, whose progeny still plough the same fields, and kneel at the same altar—the parsonage, a quaint, irregular pile, partly antiquated, but repaired, and altered in the tastes of various ages and occupants—the stile and footpath leading from the churchyard across pleasant fields, and along shady hedgerows, according to an immemorial right of way— the neighbouring village, with its venerable cottages, its public green sheltered by trees, under which the fore- fathers of the present race have sported—the antique family mansion, standing apart in some little rural domain, but looking down with a protecting air on the surrounding scene ; all these common features of English landscape evince a calm and settled security, and hereditary transmission of home-bred virtues and local attachments, that speak deeply and touchingly for the moral character of the nation.'

A generation later he is followed by another American, Nathaniel Hawthorne, and it is not too much to say that these two have done more than any con- temporary writers, with the exception of Miss Mitford, to place before us the real country life of England.

Hawthorne, indeed, sometimes found its rurality pall on him, and became a little irritated by its contented dulness. ' We saw several old villages gathered round their several churches,' he says, ' and one of these little communities, " Little Byford," had a very primitive appearance—a group of twenty or thirty dwellings of stone and thatch, without a house among them that could be so modern as a hundred years. It is a little wearisome to think of people living from century to century in the same spot, going in and out of the same doors, cultivating the same fields, meeting the same faces, and marrying one another, over and over again, and going to the same church, and lying down in the same churchyard,—to appear again and go through the same monotonous round in the next generation.' Yet if we look at it aright, it is largely to this monotony that rural England owes its restful and soothing charm.

By a curious coincidence both Dickens and Thackeray are essentially townsmen. They both write about the country, but to me they both speak merely as visitors there. In spite of the vividness of the country scenes in *Pickwick*, one feels that the writer belongs to the city. He drives through the country in the coach, and the inns are the places he knows best. There

is little of local interest in the Dickens novels;
the characters do not belong to any special locality.
These are Dickens characters, not Yorkshiremen,
or Lancashiremen, or Kentishmen. In fact, most
of them are Cockneys.

With the second half of the nineteenth century
there comes a change, for by that time the conditions
of life had altered completely. The growth of steam-
power, and the resulting spread of the factory system,
had changed England from a land of agriculturalists
and hand-workers to a great manufacturing nation,
crowded together in large cities. The old country
life, though still existing, had ceased to be the ordinary
life of the nation. It had enough of the strange
and the unusual to interest writers, and though beginning to take on the glamour that always lingers round
memories, it was there to be studied. And as the old
life fades away, more completely its associations
become dearer. Added to this, also, we have writers
now among villagers themselves, but as the writers
increase, there remains less and less that is worth
recording.

One of the first of the new school was George Eliot,
who writes on country themes with intimacy and
knowledge. Her Tullivers, and Poysers, and Cleggs

are real people, as well as being thoroughly typical of their class, and we enter into their lives, and see things from their point of view. The farm and the mill are drawn from the life, and her pages are full of clear-cut pictures.

But the writer on rural England *par excellence* is Thomas Hardy. It is his great achievement to have entered into the old life so fully, so completely, that he gives of it a rounded picture, which will remain as a record so long as English literature exists. With him we mix with men whose knowledge is not book-learning, but culled laboriously from daily experience ; whose life is under the open sky, and whose natures, simple maybe from the point of view of townfolks, have the largeness of outlook, and the poetry that comes from close association with nature. The epic of rural England one might call the Wessex novels. Where Irving and Hawthorne only saw the pictur-esque exterior, he digs deep down, and strikes the strong-flowing stream of life beneath. He sees it in its pathos and its poetry, its comedy and its tragedy, and, above all, in its essential dignity and nobility. The tragic element predominates in Hardy's work, perhaps an accident of personal temperament, perhaps because in his day the life he depicted was dying

PLATE 57. BY THE COTTAGE DOOR. REDLYNCH, WILTS.

PLATE 58. 'WHEN THE GRASS IS FULL OF FLOWERS
AND THE HEDGE IS FULL OF BOWERS'

PLATE 59. MY RABBIT

PLATE 60. COTTAGE DOOR, PARK LANE, NEAR WITLEY

PLATE 61. PEACOCK COTTAGE, WEST HORSLEY

PLATE 62. THROUGH THE CORN, DOWNTON, WILTS.

PLATE 63. OLD SURREY COTTAGE

PLATE 64. MICHAELMAS DAISIES

rapidly, and so was apt to present its more sombre side.

He strikes the keynote in the following passage: 'Winter in a solitary house in the country, without society, is tolerable, nay even enjoyable and delightful, given certain conditions. . . . These are old associa- tion—an almost exhaustive biographical or historical acquaintance with every object, animate and in- animate, within the observer's horizon. He must know all about those invisible ones of the days gone by, whose feet have traversed the fields which look so grey from his windows; recall whose creaking plough has turned those sods from time to time; whose horses and hounds have torn through that underwood; what birds affect that particular brake; what bygone domestic dramas of love, jealousy, revenge or disappointment have been enacted in the cottages, the mansions, the street, or on the green. The spot may have beauty, grandeur, salubrity, convenience, but if it lacks memories, it will ulti- mately pall upon him who settles there without opportunity of intercourse with his kind.'

And as he writes, a new world opens for us full of new conditions, new occupations, and new ideas— all of which yet are old. Who of us had any idea of the life of the forests which once spread wellnigh over all the low-lying land? But in the *Woodlanders* we are steeped in this forest lore. The roads are deep lanes, overhung with trees, not wide enough to allow two carts to pass, except at special crossing-places, and so the teams of horses are hung with a peal of bells chiming down the octave to give warning of their approach. Then the whole industry of the woodman: the bark-stripping, the felling of timber, the carting of the huge logs, the making of hurdles, of spars for thatching, and other copse ware. And most fascinating of all, the planting of the young trees.

' The holes were already dug, and they set to work. Winterbourne's fingers were endowed with a gentle conjuror's touch in spreading the roots of each little tree, resulting in a sort of caress under which the delicate fibres all laid themselves out in their proper directions for growth. He put most of these roots towards the south-west, for, he said, in forty years' time, when some great gale is blowing from that quarter, the trees will require the strongest holdfast on that side to stand against it and not fall.

' " How they sigh directly we put 'em upright, though while they are lying down they don't sigh at all," said Marty.   " Do they ? " said Giles; " I 've never noticed it."

' She erected one of the young pines into its hole, and held up her finger ; the soft, musical breathing instantly set in, which was not to cease night or day, till the grown tree should be felled—probably long after the two planters had been felled themselves.'

So the poetry of the country life reveals itself under this magician's hand. The woodlander, as we now see him, is far other than the dull rustic we took him for.   ' The casual glimpses which the ordinary population bestowed upon that wondrous world of sap and leaves had been with him a clear gaze. He had been possessed of its finer mysteries as of commonplace knowledge, had been able to read its hieroglyphs as ordinary writing. . . . From the light lashing of the twigs upon his face, when brushing through them in the dark, he would pronounce upon the species of the tree whence they stretched ; from the quality of the wind's murmur through a bough he could in like manner name its sort afar off.'   This is a knowledge of nature which is unknown to the cultured man of science, and which brings one closer to nature's heart than he can ever reach.

The last words of the epitaph on this woodlander

might stand for that of the old cottager in general, a type that had in it much that is heroic, but which is now passing só rapidly away.

' Whenever I plant the young larches, I 'll think that none can plant as you planted, and whenever I split a gad and whenever I turn the cider wring, I 'll say none could do it like you. . . . *For you was a good man and did good things.*'

CHAPTER XIV

THE COTTAGE IN PICTORIAL ART

' Every antique farmhouse and moss-grown cottage is a picture.'
WASHINGTON IRVING.

BUT while the cottage has in English literature been, until yesterday, wellnigh ignored, it has formed a theme for the pencil of the artist since the very beginnings of the English school of painting.

Perhaps the reason lies in the fact that the graphic arts are much less intellectual than the literary arts, and so choose instinctively those homely themes that appeal so directly to the feelings. Perhaps it is also that the art of landscape-painting is comparatively young and so free from the domination of classic models.

The lines on which English literature was to develop were laid down in Greece and Rome long before there was such a literary medium as the English language. The English drama, the epic, the ode, the elegy, the lyric ;—all these are based on old models.

The world of literature was old and ripe with experience before English literature was born.

Painting is a more recent art, and landscape-painting the most recent of all its branches. Modern painting begins with the Renaissance in Italy, and when a hundred and fifty years ago the English school came into existence, it was to Rome that the student turned for inspiration. ' Go to Rome and study the classics,' said Sir Joshua Reynolds, and almost every one went. But though the English school of figure-painting may be said to be based on the work of the Italian masters, notably the later Venetians, it is otherwise with our landscape-painting.

In Italy of the Renaissance, landscape-painting as an end in itself did not exist. Often in a conventionalised form it appeared in the old religious pictures, often in later work as a decorative background to portraits, as in Titian's great equestrian portrait of Charles v., but almost never as a motive in itself. At the end of the period, indeed, we have the theatrical and violent scenes of Salvator Rosa, but his was an art forced and unnatural, and he was the founder of no school. The exquisite art of Canaletto and his pupils in Venice stands in a niche by itself. Not landscape, not seascape, rather the inevitable presentment on canvas of a city so beautiful as to insist on expression, so unique in its beauty as to insist on a method of treatment of its own.

It is not to Italy but to France that we must turn for the beginnings of a classic school of landscape art in the work of Poussin and Claude, but in a sense the work of both these artists may be styled more truly Italian than French. The landscapes of Claude especially, with their effects of soft golden light, remained the model of landscape-painters for the next hundred years.

It was Claude whom Richard Wilson, the father of English landscape-painting, followed in his style. But exquisite though the art is, it is artificial and unreal. There could have been no school of English painting based on this tradition. And Wilson had little success in his own day. One can sympathise with George III. when he returned to the painter his Italianised version of Kew Gardens ; it might be classic and correct, but he, like the rest of the British public, did not wish to see his native land through those tinted spectacles. The real standpoint of the English landscape school is revealed in the answer of Constable to the connoisseur who believed in the classics, and who said, pointing to the mellow, golden varnish of an old Cremona violin, 'Here is the colour you should get in your landscapes.' The painter did not reply in words, but took the violin and laid it down on the vivid green grass of the lawn.

So when the English school arose it wanted no models, but went direct to nature, and painted English scenes as they appeared to English eyes. It was an art not of the Court, but of the people. The painters of the Court were the great portrait-painters, Reynolds, Gainsborough, Romney, and earned both wealth and fame, while the landscapists for the most part worked in obscurity, drawing-masters like Crome and Cotman, and are only now entering into their kingdom. Theirs was the conscious and deliberate selection of a humble and unpretentious theme, rather than one grandiose. Their art sprang from the deep democratic heart of the people.

And here I might digress to point out a curious parallel in the history of Japanese art. Landscape-painting there had been for hundreds of years a classic art. It dealt with nature in its most ideal and abstract form, remote from the concrete and the human. But in the end of the eighteenth century the modern spirit was at work there too, and a school of painters arose of a more democratic style. They recorded scenes of everyday life, and were called painters of 'the Passing World.' And Hokusai and Hiroshiye, the two great landscape-painters of this school, depicted not abstract scenes, but toured the country and placed its beauty-spots on record. Fuji, the sacred mountain, appeared in Hokusai's famous series of prints, the 'Thirty-six Views of Fuji.' A series of bridges and of waterfalls followed. Art had descended from its seat in the heavens and come down among the people.

So far as the English landscapist had a model, they found it in the quiet but searching work of the old Dutch and Flemish painters, Teniers, Ruisdael, Hobbema, and Ostade. The flat landscapes of their native land delighted these simple painters; where the human interest entered, village and rural life supplied the theme, and often forming a background to the merry figure groups, or itself forming the centre of a landscape composition, was a rustic cottage, like and yet unlike its English neighbours. Hobbema especially realised to the full the beauty of such subjects; his old mills, with their grey timber-work, are studied with care and depicted with a loving touch. Even the great master, Rembrandt, treated such simple themes, and under his magic hand they assumed a great breadth and dignity, till the peasant's cottage was as impressive as the prince's palace. More so, for the first seems to take on the largeness of its natural surroundings, while the latter cannot so lose itself in the larger unity, but remains self-assertive but insignificant.

In landscape the subject often stands for little, while the treatment is everything. In the impressionist art of Monet, two haystacks served as the theme for numerous studies, each one a different picture, and based on the changing aspects of light. But the old method was more ingenuous. Passing, and what we might call accidental, effects excited little interest in the mind of the painter; it was more the innate qualities of the subject that preoccupied him. In the new style the artist would miss success if he allowed the underlying subject to assert itself strongly; it would overpower his real theme, the effect of light, or of colour, as the case might be. But in the old style the more distinctly observed, and the more deliberately rendered the subject, the better, for it itself formed the theme of the picture. A cottage to the older school was not merely a mass of tone, a patchwork of glorious colour, but a thing made by human hands, full of the evidence of human thought.

Everywhere it spoke of years of human occupation, and it bore visibly on its face the signs of its battle with the elements, wind, and sun, and rain. Such a picture was in a sense a historic document, and whatever the merits of the rival schools, it is undeniable that the older is that which appeals to the larger public.

Gainsborough is the first English painter who struck the homely and natural note in his landscapes. Of him we might almost say, that he was a portrait-painter by profession, but a landscape-painter by nature. Influenced to some extent by the Dutch masters, his style is yet thoroughly English. He went direct to nature for his subjects, and painted them with sympathy and affection, and with a fine sense of their pictorial qualities. In his early studies of Suffolk landscapes, there is a freshness and a fidelity to nature that are something quite new, but one almost regrets his success as a portrait-painter, as it left him less and less time for landscape work, and his later landscapes are more in the nature of studio compositions, painted from his early recollections, than direct studies.

It was the decorative aspect of nature that appealed to him, rather than the details of its rural life, and in

the well-known 'Cottage Door,' the cottage itself
does not take a prominent part in the picture. It is
a mere suggestion, a doorway and a thatched roof,
buried beneath the shade of heavy trees. The interest
is concentrated on the group of rather artificial
figures at the door, and the somewhat theatrical
effect of the picture is enhanced by a blasted tree,
which stretches up its bare limbs to the sky. In some
of Gainsborough's slighter chalk sketches, however,
the cottage appears in more familiar guise.

Morland, who followed in the next generation,
dealt with rural subjects in a much closer and more
intimate way, and perhaps there never was a great
painter who suited more exactly the tastes of his
patrons. For Morland in his tastes and his habits
was cut out, not for the life of the cultivated man
about town, but for that of the country squire. A
fine horseman, he rode as a jockey at Margate ; his
pleasures were those of the tavern, his favourite
companions stable-boys. In refined society he was
always ill at ease ; but happy-go-lucky, generous, and
hearty, he was a hero among his boon companions.
And even this career of pot-house dissipation, a
continual round of low pleasures, though it sapped
his magnificent constitution and brought him to an

early grave at the age of forty-one, yet in one way served his turn better than any other could. In his paintings of country inns, stables, and barns, with the horses, dogs, and attendant rustics, he is dealing with the life he knows thoroughly, the only life he sympathises with, and understands. However careless his work, it is never hesitating; he knows exactly what he wishes to say, though sometimes slovenly enough in the way of saying it. His old country inns are real inns, his countrymen observed from the life, his horses and dogs he knew as one knows his best friends, and his cottages are the actual homes of the people. For he flattered no one, and painted things just as they are. But while his horses, and dogs, and men are individuals, his cottages and trees are rather apt to be merely types. For he rarely painted such things direct from nature, but in the studio and chiefly from memory.

Mention must be made, too, of that wonderful draughtsman and most prolific worker, Thomas Rowlandson, to whom we owe such a life-like portrait of Morland.

In the numberless drawings of wagoners and their teams, of coaches, and horses, of oxen, of village inns, which he dashed off with such astonishing dexterity and sureness, we have all the characteristics of the old cottage, depicted with an unerring hand. His types, too, are living men and women, and touched in with wonderful spirit. And he possessed, too, that wonderful instinct for composition, that feeling for delicate balance, which makes his slightest sketch a picture.

Contemporary with Morland flourished the group of men who made the English school of landscape-painting. Of these the two greatest were Crome and Constable. Crome, the founder of the Norwich school, is a painter who only now is receiving his due meed of appreciation. Quiet and unobtrusive, he taught drawing and painting for a living, and painted landscape for pleasure. His canvases are full of vastness and dignity, the feeling of the open air, but he is less intimate in his feeling for rural life than Constable. 'I love,' said the latter, 'every stile, and stump, and lane in the village ; as long as I am able to hold a brush, I shall never cease to paint them.' And he found his themes near at home. The mill, the cottage, the farmhouse, those were his favourite subjects. He was the first man to paint truly the greenness and moisture of England, its showery skies, with their swiftly changing clouds. And he treated the old English cottage with the familiarity of perfect knowledge and sympathy. In the 'Valley Farm,' in the National Gallery, we have a perfect picture of the English homestead. The old house, the very embodiment of ease and comfort, with big outside chimney, and the whitewash peeling off the walls here and there in big flakes. It is set in a real English landscape, great trees enfold the house, and in the foreground is a pool of water with cattle. The sky is blue, with great puffs of white fleecy clouds, which reflect the sunshine with dazzling brightness. It looks as though a shower had just cleared off, and the whole landscape was basking in the sun, refreshed by its bath. The air is full of moisture and the smell of damp earth. It is not an ideal landscape, but a picture of an actual scene. The farmhouse is on the banks of the Stour near Hatford Mill, and was known as 'Willy Lott's house.' Willy Lott, its possessor, was born in the house, and lived there for more than eighty years, without having spent four whole days away from it. The subject was a favourite one with Constable. A different view of the house appears in the 'Hay Wain.'

And while in oil Constable painted these homely subjects in a way that has never been surpassed, a school of English water-colour was growing up, treating landscape from the natural point of view of Constable and Crome, but with a delicacy and purity which is the special charm of their medium. It was in this school that Turner learned the mastery of his craft, which he afterwards turned to such audacious use, and there are those who prefer his earlier and less ambitious efforts, to the bewildering canvases of his later days. And associated with him were Thomas Girtin, whose brilliant promise was frustrated by his early death, John Sell Cotman, John Varley, Copley Fielding, Peter de Wint, David Cox, and many others.

Of these we may single out especially David Cox and Peter de Wint as having made their own English rural and domestic scenes. Indeed, the drawing-books published by David Cox were full of studies of old cottages and farms, and probably did more than any other agency to popularise this style of subject. From Jane Austen's pages we learn that it was part of the education of every accomplished young lady that she should be taught to portray with her pencil such scenes as a picturesque cottage or a fallen tree.

It was in Wales that Cox chiefly found his subjects,

and De Wint in Lincolnshire, but both painted the old cottage with a sympathetic hand, and entered with zest into all the changes of the rural year. Cox's water-mills, and De Wint's harvest-fields are especially characteristic, and of the latter we have two fine examples in South Kensington Museum, full of the glory of yellow corn, with the huddled roofs of cottages and the spire of the village church in the distance.

Such a style of art has taken firm root in England. The preference for homely subjects, the direct treatment, the sympathy for rural life, these are the qualities seen in much of the best of our landscape, and this is the art which awakens the readiest echoes in the heart of the people. In landscape, at least, the days of the classic schools are over ; pedantry interests no one. At the other extreme, the impressionists, preoccupied with effects of light and colour which have a strongly scientific basis, and the decorative landscapists, to whom the pattern in line or colour is the end for which the subject is merely an excuse, do not appeal to more than a small section.

In the Victorian era, amid much that is only commonplace, we find one or two men who treated those simple subjects with distinction. Among these

Birket Foster occupies a niche of his own. In his water-colours, and perhaps still more in his black-and-white drawings, the cottage forms a favourite theme. But in his hands it is invested with a wonderful dignity. The draughtsmanship is admirable; the essentials of the old buildings are seized and set down with an unerring touch, and despite the wealth of detail the feeling of the whole is broad, almost grand. Above all, the artist possesses the supreme gift of composition, placing each object inevitably in its proper relation to the rest till the whole is an organic unity, and has the magic quality of a living thing.

Fred Walker, too, did not disdain those simple dwellings, and the cottages in the neighbourhood of his home at Cookham figure in many of his paintings. Their exquisite colour, the classic grace of the figures, and the loving detail lavished on tree and plant and flower, made them the delight of art lovers a generation ago, but to-day, alas, hidden, for the most part, in private collections, they are but seldom seen.

Mention must also be made of George Mason, his contemporary, who treated rural subjects with a sensitive feeling that is full of charm.

In Mrs. Helen Allingham, reproductions of whose drawings illustrate this volume, we have in our own day an artist who has made the old cottage a theme peculiarly her own.

She studied first at the Birmingham School of Design, but entered the Academy Schools in 1867, where she had the advantage of the advice of such men as Millais, Leighton, and Fred Walker.

Her first work was chiefly in black and white, and during her student career she supplied drawings to *Once a Week*, *Little Folks*, and other illustrated journals. Shortly after the *Graphic* started on its successful career in 1870, she was asked to contribute to its pages, and for some years drawings from her hand continued to appear there regularly. She also illustrated Thomas Hardy's *Far from the Madding Crowd* on its first publication, anonymously, in *Cornhill*.

In 1874 she married William Allingham, the poet, and from that time began to devote herself more to work in colour.

For the first seven years of her married life her home was in London, and during that time her figure-studies, chiefly of rural subjects, became more and more known. In 1875 she entered the Royal Water-colour Society, becoming a full member in 1890, when for the first time a woman had that privilege.

The year after Miss Clara Montalba was made a member.

In 1881 her home was shifted to Sandhills, near Witley in Surrey, right in the midst of the most delightful rural scenery in England, a move which had a far-reaching effect upon her art. From that time is dated the series of delightful studies of old English cottages upon which her reputation rests. At first the figures in her drawings were the more important feature, and the cottage the less, but as time went on the cottage increased in importance, till the real subject was the study of an old English home.

A member of the Old Water-colour Society, Mrs. Allingham belongs, alike in her sympathies and her methods, to the old school of water-colour painting, based on the traditions of the masters of a hundred years ago. When the modern impressionist would turn his flash-light on the cottage, and paint it as a blaze of red brick thatched with gold, she brings a quietly contemplative gaze to bear upon it, and under her unobtrusive hand, the old building reveals to us something of its history. When he would see nothing but the play of sunlight on the varying surfaces, and strain the resources of his palette to achieve the impossible, and transfer this light to his canvas, she realises the feeling of calm domesticity which has spread over the scene, and so this, too, finds its way into her painting. And it is to this home feeling, this sympathy with rural life in all its forms, that her work owes much of the charm which has made it so deservedly popular. The cottage to her is not a dead thing, merely an excuse for brilliant passages in paint, but almost a living thing, bearing imprinted upon it all sorts of interesting facts regarding its character and history. She sees in it the essence of the old English country life. The old woman in her white cap stands in the doorway, the fresh young wife dandles her baby in her arms, the pigeons cluster on the red-tiled roof, and the children play about the garden gate.

It is curious how much temperament affects an artist's work, and Mrs. Allingham's outlook is essentially a cheerful one. It is noticeable that in all the sixty or more illustrations to this volume, there is not a single dark or lowering sky. Her England is a sunny England, her cottages are happy homes. One can imagine those cottages painted in quite a different way. The old twisted beams could be made to look grim and terrible, the building unutterably sad in its decay. One can see it on a tract of desolate waste land, the winds of winter howling round it, wet and sodden, a picture of discomfort. But her cottages have always a green and smiling old age. The garden is full of flowers, the sun shines with a cool and tempered light, and the whole scene breathes of peacefulness. There is no jarring note. Where the modern occupier has erected an ugly iron railing, or cut through the beams of the framework in enlarging a window, or added a corrugated iron roof to a lean-to, a judicious restoration has taken place, and we see the cottage not as it unfortunately now is, but as it used to be. Her women wear the sunbonnets and her men the smocks of another day, and so the picture is complete.

In the plate of a Surrey cottage facing page 146,[1] we find a typical specimen of Mrs. Allingham's work at its best. The first thing that strikes one about it is the extreme delicacy and refinement of its colouring, the silver-grey of the timbers, the light clear reds of the brick walls, contrasting with the darker hue of the mossy tiles, the gay colours of the flower-garden, the lissom figure of the girl with the clothes-basket, the fresh greens of the foreground, and the greyer greens of the distant trees, and above,

1. Plate 33 in this edition

the cool, airy sky; it forms at once a homely and a dainty picture.

But underlying this pleasing general effect there is an extreme care in observing and accuracy in recording every feature. Every twist of the old oak beams is shown, every curve in the roof, for it has sunk down on the rafters, so that the rows of tiles undulate like ripples on a sandy shore. Even the tiles themselves are not put in haphazard; the rows are counted. All the little eccentricities of form which give character, and endear those cottages to us, are faithfully delineated. The gable roof, just above the main roof, not on the same level; the little gablet at the other end, above the little hip roof; the courses of brick round the foot of the chimneys, the one just a little lower than the other; the contrast of the ridge tile with the flat tile—everything is there. In the garden border, too, one can pick out the various flowers.

Equally beautiful as a drawing, and much finer as a building, is the cottage near Haslemere, facing the next page, so simple in plan, yet of such extreme elegance, with its high-pitched roof, covered with lichen of grey and gold, and richly wrought chimney-tops. I have heard it said that such steep pitched roofs were all originally thatched, and that the tiles are a quite recent innovation. This may be so in many cases, and an examination of the tiles might settle each case; in this instance I should not be inclined to think so, for the following reason. At the base of each chimney a course of bricks juts out. These are not merely ornamental, decorative though their effect is, but are designed to throw off the rain, and prevent it soaking in at the junction of roof and chimney. Now this course of brick is just above the surface of the tiles. A thatched roof would bury it completely and render it useless. The elegance of the chimney precludes any possibility of its being a recent addition, and we are forced to the conclusion that roof and chimney were built at the same time. Probably the truth is that the builder, in this case, merely adopted the high-pitched roof suitable for thatch, on account of its beauty of form, for there are many instances of architectural forms surviving from their decorative qualities long after their original use has ceased.

It is in this district round about Haslemere, Witley, and Godalming that Mrs. Allingham has done much of her best work.

After the daintiness and elegance of these Surrey

cottages, the more primitive thatched structures of Wiltshire and Hampshire seem somewhat shapeless, though the cool grey roof harmonises well with the greens of the trees. There always seems to me, however, to be a lack of character about the thatched roof; its rather blanket-like folds are too thick to act as drapery, and indicate the form beneath, and they have not sufficient rigidity to acquire lines of their own of any decision.

Nothing, however, could be more charming than the series of little thatched cottages from the Isle of Wight. These stone-built, one-storied cottages have all the primitive qualities that one meets with in the Scotch Highlands, but with little touches of ornament added to chimney, and round the door and windows, for which one would look there in vain.

Of the more detailed drawings, very interesting are the two of cottage doorways facing pages 244 and 264.[1] The first, with its life-like group at the door, the children, and the kindly old woman ' somdale stepe in age,' is a charming study. Through the ivy that smothers roof and walls we get a glimpse of mullioned windows, beehives stand on a little home-made bench, and the borders are gay with pansies and wallflowers.

1. Plates 56 and 60 in this edition

In the second, we get a closer view of an old door-way. The door is not built in panels, but of match-boarding in the old-fashioned way; a big oak beam supports the wall above it, and the doorstep is fitted together like a puzzle with small slabs of flat stone.

Another excellent drawing is the characteristic Kentish village street, so silvery in its colouring, with its long broken line of irregular roofs, the tiles all green with moss.

In her landscape studies of the Downs and the Weald, the artist shows the same delicacy of feeling and of touch.   It is not so much the larger aspects of those great stretches of plain that appeal to her as their tender distances, the green woods fading off into faint blues and purples and greys, while the fore-ground is spread with nature's carpet of wild flowers.

This love of flowers is seen in the rendering of many cottage gardens, and also finds fuller expression in the delightful studies painted in a garden which, even among Surrey gardens, is famous, for it has grown under the loving care of one who has found the garden a lifelong solace and delight, and whose writings on that subject are known by all who value garden lore.   And of these studies, the best of all seems to me that of the Michaelmas daisies, with its background of soft greens, against which blaze the flower masses, white, pale blue, faint purples, and soft reds.

But it is by her cottage pictures that Mrs. Allingham's name has been made a household word; it is in them, rather than in the landscapes or flower subjects, that we find her best work, and it is by them that she will be most fittingly remembered.

INDEX

THE END